Inclusive Education isn't Dead, it Just Smells Funny

T0316337

Positing inclusive education as a cornerstone of democracy, social equality and effective education, this unique book offers a timely response to the recent conservative backlash which has dismissed inclusive education as a field of research and practice which has become outdated and unfit for purpose.

With profound insight and clarity, Slee delves deep into the architecture of modern-day schooling to show how inclusive education has been misappropriated and subverted, manifesting itself in a culture of ableism, an ethic of competitive individualism and the illusion of *special educational needs*. A unique book in both form and content, the author draws on music and art theory, on real-life observations and global experience, contemporary education policy and practice to reject calls for a return to segregated schooling, and put forward a compelling counterargument for schooling which models the kind of world we want our children to live in – a world of authentic, rather than divided communities.

A timely response to a modern-day debate with global relevance, *Inclusive Education isn't Dead, it Just Smells Funny* will be of interest to researchers and educators, policy makers, parents and practitioners with an interest in inclusive education.

Roger Slee is Professor at the School of Education, University of South Australia. He is Founding Editor of the *International Journal of Inclusive Education* and has published widely over the course of a long and distinguished career.

Inclusive Education isn't Dead, it Just Smells Funny

Roger Slee

Routledge
Taylor & Francis Group

LONDON AND NEW YORK

First published 2018
by Routledge

2 Park Square, Milton Park, Abingdon, Oxfordshire OX14 4RN
52 Vanderbilt Avenue, New York, NY 10017

Routledge is an imprint of the Taylor & Francis Group, an informa business

First issued in paperback 2019

Routledge is an imprint of the Taylor & Francis Group, an informa business

British Library Cataloguing-in-Publication Data
A catalogue record for this book is available from the British Library

Library of Congress Cataloging-in-Publication Data
Names: Slee, Roger, author.
Title: Inclusive education isn't dead, it just smells funny /
   Roger Slee.
Description: New York : Routledge, [2018] | Includes
   bibliographical references and index.
Identifiers: LCCN 2018009390 (print) |
   LCCN 2018012712 (ebook) | ISBN 9780429486869 (eb) |
   ISBN 9781138597617 (hb: alk. paper)
Subjects: LCSH: Inclusive education.
Classification: LCC LC1200 (ebook) | LCC LC1200 .S53 2018
   (print) | DDC 371.9/046—dc23
LC record available at https://lccn.loc.gov/2018009390

ISBN: 978-1-138-59761-7 (hbk)
ISBN: 978-0-367-85606-9 (pbk)

Typeset in Times New Roman
by Apex CoVantage, LLC

For Felix and Lila

Contents

Acknowledgements

This book is formed by more than a sequence of words. It has lived in my head and in conversations with friends and acquaintances for a long time. As a result, there are many people to thank. So many people influence your work over time – some directly, others in circuitous, peripheral and incidental, but important ways. Listing these people would be too difficult, so I am offering a general vote of thanks.

More specifically I would like to thank Stephen Ball for our many chats in Balham coffee houses over the years about writing. Al Luke is always on the end of the phone when you need to interrogate music, life and social theory, in that order. Mel Ainscow and Dan Goodley read a near-complete draft of the book, and their encouragement was most welcome.

Thank you to Sally Tomlinson for agreeing to write her splendid foreword despite her extremely hectic "retirement" schedule. Sally Tomlinson, Len Barton and Mike Oliver established the foundations from which our work proceeds.

Special thanks to Michael Leunig for allowing me to use his wonderful cartoons (art). Like many Australians I grew up with his work close by.

Tim Corcoran was supremely patient as our collaborative writing was constantly deferred until the manuscript was finished. Gordon Tait also kindly delayed the commencement of our next writing project.

Thanks to Stephen Dobson and colleagues at the University of South Australia for their support.

Thanks, as always, to Jeanette, Carly, Rowan, Lauren and Hendrik. And to Felix Rocky and Lila Ruby – I hope that you and your contemporaries are up to the challenges we have sadly left for you.

There were so many musicians who Poppy and I listened to while in the workroom. This project drew heavily from them, as do I, for sustenance in an increasingly troubled world.

Finally, thanks to Alison Foyle at Routledge for her advocacy and sup-port, and to Elsbeth Wright for her care with the manuscript. I remain thankful to Malcolm Clarkson and Anna Clarkson for their early interest in my work.

Roger Slee
Melbourne, February 2018.

Foreword

In 1864 the Right Honourable Earl of Zetland, KT, the Most Worshipful Master of the Freemasons of England, laid the foundation stone for the Royal Albert Asylum for Idiots and Imbeciles of the Northern Counties in England. One potential inmate, included in the audience, was so excited by the occasion that he had to be chained to a barrel. In 2018, it was reported that children in German schools 'diagnosed' with Attention Deficit Hyperactivity Disorder (ADHD) were made to wear vests filled with sand, sometimes referred to as compression vests or squeeze jackets, to keep them in their seats in class. One teacher who was enthusiastic about the sand vests was the Head of the Inclusion Unit at Grumbechstrasse School in Hamburg.[1] Weighing children down with sand was apparently a gentler form of therapy than keeping them quiet with drugs. So, do we celebrate these versions of inclusion? The chained young man will spend his life excluded from society in an asylum. The children clothed in sand are already excluded in an 'Inclusion Unit' in their school. So, are chains, sand and drugs acceptable ways of 'including' children and young people?

Or, as Beck would have it, 'the world is unhinged', and the language of inclusion, beloved over the past forty years by politicians, administrators, practitioners and some academics has indeed become a crazy contortion of what is really happening. Are all of these contorted inclusive practices just elaborate ways of masking the exclusion of young people who are considered as disabled, disruptive, and have learning difficulties or any of the myriad other labels given to those 'not quite normal'? After all, to get rid of the 'not normal' makes life smoother for the normal.

Roger Slee has devoted his life as a teacher, administrator and academic to showing up the madness in the ways societies which call themselves civilized treat those whose differences cannot apparently be accommodated in daily life. As colleagues at Goldsmiths' College, London in the 1990s, he and I swapped stories of how the madness was enacted. He told me how, as a young teacher, he found himself chasing a young girl who had 'escaped' from a school for the maladjusted and, trying to prise her hands from their grip on fence railings she clung to while sobbing, he tried to reassure onlookers that it was OK because he was a teacher. I told him that just a few weeks back near the college, a young black man had fallen in an epileptic fit in a shop, and the other customers had backed away in fear. And I remembered the little boy who early in my teaching career had been at a school for 'problem children', who told me solemnly that he had "been to the sea-side". It turned out he had paddled in drain water by the road. His parents were too poor to go on any sea-side holiday. He didn't know the exclusions visited on him then and later were due to a society that tolerated high levels of poverty and found ways of telling the poor that they were deficient. Naturally we shared our outrage when Herrnstein and Murray's[2] fallacious book *The Bell Curve: Intelligence and Class Structure in American Life* was published in 1994. It stands as a monument to the abhorrent foundations of psychometrics.

In his writing over the years, Roger has made it his major task to interrogate the sloganized clichés that the term 'inclusive education' now trades on. It is no wonder, as he has noted, *"that students register confusion and even fear as they find themselves trying to navigate a field which appears simultaneously treacherous, exclusionary and illusive".*[3] They were not helped by the antagonistic and often vitriolic attacks by those who felt it was right to exclude children in special schools, units and classes, and those who began to criticise exclusionary practices. But over the years the exclusionists developed a cunning plan! They would take over the concept of inclusion and arrange an education system that excluded as far as possible, and in a variety of ways, the disabled, disruptive, those with learning problems, lower-class poor children, many racial and ethnic minority children, and rather more boys than girls – boys usually growing up to be more troublesome. But all this would take place in the name of a benevolent inclusion. Then these 'included' children could go on to be included in vocational courses and if lucky, lower-level jobs, or cared for in 'homes', or by poorly paid carers, or of course, in prisons where many recipients of special educational programmes eventually find themselves. And, all this while claiming good, inclusive intentions! As John Richardson and his colleagues have pointed out, *"the practices reflect the long-term continuity of benevolence as a form of social and cultural control directed to the problems that arise from the economically poor and marginal and the physically and mentally vulnerable".*[4]

But now, as Roger notes in this book and in his own inimitable way, the phoney inclusionists may have been rumbled. The slippery concept of inclusive education has begun to smell a little like something decaying, maybe a dead rabbit by the road which didn't run fast enough. If, as he writes at the end of this book, you sit in a room listening to parents who speak with quiet despair and suppressed anger about how they tried and failed to secure an inclusive education for their children, and of the many schools which do not want them, you start to wonder whether inclusive education is still alive. Maybe it would be more honest now to confess that some societies, especially the economically unequal ones, really want a hierarchical education system, which reproduces itself by sponsoring the children of the elites into elite positions. Market competition to produce the 'best' schools, placated by forms of selection for the 'more able', and residual education for the less able, the disruptive and the disabled – categories which usually include the poor and many minorities – excludes them from comfortable life chances.

The *Roger Way* (as I call it) of making readers think about what is actually going on, combines erudite knowledge, humour and a deep compassion for the human race, in which all individuals are 'deficient' in some way or other. It is not often you find a book which in the first essay mentions Adam Smith and his Theories of Moral Sentiments, Donald Trump and his trumping about a 'Crippled America' and a discussion of the musical theories of jazz musician Frank Zappa. It helps to know that Roger is a jazz musician as well as a professor. Readers will find here an unusual and thought-provoking text, meant to disturb received wisdom and unthinking acceptance of moral cruelties. Enjoy the essays and the interludes which, like the blind man with the lamp, illuminate much of what is going on in the name of inclusion.

Sally Tomlinson
Oxford, 1 February 2018.

Notes

1 Connolly, K. (2018) "Use of sand vests to calm children with ADHD sparks controversy in Germany." *The Guardian*, London, January 20th.
2 Herrnstein, R. J. and Murray C. A. (1994) *The bell curve: intelligence and class structure in American life*. London: Simon & Schuster.
3 Allan, J. and Slee, R. (2008) *Doing inclusive educational research*. Rotterdam, The Netherlands: Sense Publishers, page 3.
4 Richardson, J. G., Wu, J. and Judge, D. M. (2017) *The global convergence of vocational and special education*. New York and London: Routledge.

Exposition

Exclusion resides deep in the bones of education. Like any metastases, sites of origin are not always obvious. This makes detection and treatment difficult. Without wanting to belabour or render gratuitous, the cancer metaphor, though a cancer it is, we know that exclusion, as a social phenomenon, is a stubborn foe. After all, *antiquity* and *ubiquity* are the agents of its resilience.[1] And, it seems that our interventions to dismantle it or minimise its effects at best seem to have minimal impact and, at worst, strengthen and sustain it.

We could say that exclusion is an ontological given, a part of our social, and therein our educational, DNA or *zeitgeist*. The paradox is, as Zygmunt Bauman[2] instructed, that we live in a liquid time where community is precarious and estrangement is endemic and yet public discourses are littered with utterances of inclusion. Expressions of *ambient fear*[3] were once veiled; they lurked in the political undergrowth. Political landscapes change and with it so too the lexicons of public debate.[4] Hate is no longer whispered; its pitch is loud and shrill. For as Toni Morrison who was awarded the Nobel Prize for Literature in 1993 tells us with elegant force:

> "*Why should we want to know the stranger when it is easier to estrange another? Why should we want to close the distance when we can close the gate?*"[5]

The Trump presidency, undersigned by fear and loathing, is building a social imaginary of national fortification, banishment of the immigrant, and derision of the basic principles of fairness. Trump's election policy guidebook is forged in an ableist discourse. *Crippled America: How to Make America Great Again*[6] "*offers the ugliest example of what became a pattern of ableist language over the course of his campaign*".[7]

The prescience of Adam Smith writing in the 1700s in *The Theory of Moral Sentiment* is astonishing:

> *This disposition to admire, and almost to worship, the rich and the powerful, and to despise, or, at least, to neglect persons of poor and mean condition, though necessary both to establish and to maintain the distinction of ranks and the order of society, is, at the same time, the great and most universal cause of the corruption of our moral sentiment.*[8]

Of course, Trump represents what has been brewing for some time.[9] *Golden Dawn* in Greece, Marine Le Pen and the shadow of her now-impossible-to-extricate shadow of the *National Front* in France, Geert Wilders' *Party for Freedom* in the Netherlands, Pauline Hanson's *One Nation Party* in Australia, and the *Danish People's Party* are but a few of the destinations bookmarked on a *Lonely Planet* tour of this resurgence of extreme, and increasingly respectable, right politics. Each of these parties self-describes as representing the people and setting forth a chance to rebuild sovereign nations free from the threat of the waves of displaced people from the Middle East, the horn of Africa and Eastern Europe. Camus and Lebourg's analysis in *Far-Right Politics in Europe* counsel caution in the representation and reduction of the far-right political movements we are witnessing.[10] I would not be the only commentator to suggest that there is a sense of what has gone before. Social amnesia is a pandemic that sweeps aside the legacy of a Europe of little over 80 years ago.[11]

In true Hegelian form, Zizek reminds us that these *disparities* reflect the presence of the negative deep within the weave of those things we offer as fundamental positives.[12] It's not a case of good co-existing with evil, but more a case of evil lurking deep within good. That which it commissions preys on the essence of democracy: freedom of speech, movement and association. Classic expressions of democracy condemn us to "*defend to the death*" the right to freedom of expression for those who would tear democracy, and freedom itself, apart.[13] **When our foundational beliefs are threatened, we must not capitulate. We must redouble our efforts to restore that which we believe in.**

Alas, Mister Dickens, these are the worst of times with little mitigation. Our sensibilities are dulled in an age of banality. There is an unprecedented level of displacement of people by conflict, by so-called *natural* disasters that arrive with greater frequency as markers of the '*shock of the Anthropocene*',[14] by political persecution and by the ravages of poverty. To seek refuge from imminent danger, to invite the kindness of strangers, is to invoke the ire of respectable politics. In a recent concert in Melbourne, the English musician and erstwhile political activist Billy Bragg reminded the audience that while we shake our heads with collective disapproval of Trump and his wall, walls are common, bridges not so. The English stop refugees at the French coastline, the Europeans subsidise the Turks to contain the human traffic from Syria and Australians will pay anyone to process asylum seekers offshore.

In his posthumously published work, *The Metamorphosis of the World*, Ulrich Beck attempts perspective in his preface:

> *The world is unhinged. As many people see it, this is true in both senses of the word: the world is out of joint and it has gone mad. We are wandering aimlessly and confused, arguing for this and against that. But a statement on which most people can agree, beyond all antagonisms and across all continents, is: "I don't understand the world anymore".*[15]

Let us follow his thinking a little further. He writes:

> *This book represents an attempt to rescue myself, and perhaps others too, from a major embarrassment. Even though I teach sociology and studying the transformation of modern societies for many years, I was at a loss for an answer to the simple but necessary question 'What is the meaning of the global events unfolding before our eyes on the television', and I was forced to declare bankruptcy. There was nothing – neither a concept nor a theory – capable of expressing the turmoil of this world as required by the German philosopher Hegel.*[16]

I didn't set out to commence this book in anger. I have and now I must return to my task. However, some emotions are difficult to suppress, and they will surface at various times in the pages that follow. Perhaps this is exactly what is required – the putting aside of the civility which is, after all is said and done, an incubus for exclusion? Why do we not, as Tony Booth said in a recent conversation, consistently call our colleagues to account for their conceptual flabbiness when they indulge in the ableist language of special educational needs?

In this brief exposition, I reluctantly offer exclusion as a reinvigorated metaphor for our times. This book adjusts its focus from exclusion as a general social condition to the particular plight of children and young people with disabilities, along with their families and advocates, as they attempt to secure the legislative right to an inclusive education. The discourse of policy texts from many education jurisdictions headlines their commitment to the principles and practice of inclusive education. The lines from these scripts have been rehearsed and recited by educators across all quarters. It has become an empty language. Monitoring Committees for the implementation of the United Nations Convention on the Rights of Persons with Disabilities, in their reviews of the progress of signatory countries, attest to a reluctance even to minimum compliance expectations.[17] Together with government and non-government reviews of education for students with disabilities,[18] there is a growing body of evidence reminding us of systematic exclusion of students with disabilities.[19]

How you read this book is up to you. I usually write cover to cover, but not this time. Instead, I wanted to write a book in the manner of a musical composition with an opening *exposition, interludes* between the three major essays or *movements* and finally a *coda*. The three essays, which are connected by interludes, may be consumed as stand-alone pieces – almost complete offerings in themselves – or you may receive the work from start to end. The platform from which the work proceeds is an interrogation of inclusive education as we near the end of this second decade of the twenty-first century. Characteristically my exploration of inclusion takes shape through an examination of exclusion. The three essays: *A Time for Frank Speaking; Perspective, Illusions and Other Treacheries*; and *Diving for Dear Life* stand, or fall, as provocations for better theory and practice in an area of social policy that has an inconsistent – no, a dismal – track record. Children with disabilities are too often, in Bauman's terms, the *surplus population* of education. They inhabit the margins of schooling, looking on at the education main game. We ought to be able to do better than this. In her chilling account of violence against children in *Killing Daniel*, Daniel Helen Garner reflects on the shadow of shame that this "worm in the heart of the rose" casts over us all.[20] Are we also going to allow inclusive education to remain a *"bleak story of moral paralysis and missed opportunities"*?[21]

Notes

1 I came across this couplet in Daniel Levitin's book *The world in six songs* where he in fact borrowed it from the musicologist David Huron to describe the insinuation of music into our everyday lives. Like Daniel I was taken by its expansive utility and applied it to the task of analysing social exclusion in a book called *The Irregular School*.

2 See Zygmunt Bauman (2004) *Wasted lives: modernity and its outcasts*. Cambridge: Polity; and Bauman, Z. (2016) *Strangers at our door*. Cambridge: Polity.

3 Bauman (2004) *Wasted lives*.

4 This process of discursive shifts is tracked by Norman Fairclough (2000) in *New labour, new language*. London: Routledge and elaborated by Stephen Ball (2007) in *Education plc*. London: Routledge.

5 Morrison, T. (2017) *The origin of others*. Cambridge, MA: Harvard University Press, page 38.

6 Trump, Donald. (2015) *Crippled America: how to make America great again*. New York: Threshold Editions.

7 Harnish, A. (2017) Ableism and the trump phenomenon. *Disability & Society*, 32(3): 423–428.
8 I recently read this quote as an epigraph in Zygmunt Bauman's (2013) *Does the richness of the few benefit us all?* Cambridge: Polity. The quote is from Smith, A. (1759) *The theory of moral sentiment*. Part 1, Chapter 3. www.marxists.org/reference/archive/smith-adam/works/moral/part01/part1c.htm.
9 See for example: Apple, M. W. (2001) *Educating the "right" way: markets, standards, God, and inequality*. London: Routledge Falmer.
10 Camus, J-Y. and Lebourg, N. (2017) *Far-right politics in Europe*. London: The Bellknapp Press of Harvard University Press.
11 As I write, seated at a table in the Brotherton Library in Leeds following a terrorist bomb attack at a concert arena in Manchester, attacks on pedestrians with a large van mounting the footpath on London Bridge and knife attacks on patrons in a hotel in Borough, fear of 'foreigners', though for the main part we speak of young people born in or long-time residents of Britain swells.
12 Zizek, S. (2016) *Disparities*. London: Bloomsbury.
13 Here I refer to the quote that is popularly attributed to Voltaire, but was actually composed by Evelyn Beatrice Hall, writing as S. G. Tallentyne, in The Friends of Voltaire (1906). "I disapprove of what you say, but I will defend to the death your right to say it."
14 Bonneuil, C. and Fressoz, J-B. (2017) *The shock of the anthropocene*. London: Verso.
15 Beck, U. (2016) *The metamorphosis of the world*. Cambridge: Polity, page 1.
16 Ibid., page 3.
17 See for example: ***Australia UNCRPD Committee Report 2013*** "The Committee is concerned that despite the Disability Standards for Education established to ensure access to education on an equal basis, students with disabilities continue to be placed in special schools and many of those who are in regular schools are largely confined to special classes or units. The Committee is further concerned that students with disabilities enrolled in regular schools receive a substandard education due to lack of reasonable accommodation. The Committee is also concerned that secondary school completion rates for students with disabilities are about half of those for people without disability." ***New Zealand UNCRPD Committee Report 2014*** "The Committee notes the steps being taken to increase inclusive primary and secondary education, and the ongoing challenges to making the education system fully inclusive, such as the lack of reasonable accommodation. The Committee is concerned at reports indicating that children with disabilities experience bullying in schools, and notes that there is no enforceable right to inclusive education." ***UK UNCRC Committee Report 2016***: "The Committee is concerned that: (a) Many children with disabilities do not see that their views are given due weight in making personal decisions in their life, including choice of support and future; (b) Many children with disabilities are still placed in special schools or special units in mainstream schools and many school buildings and facilities are not made fully accessible to children with disabilities; (c) Provision of the support for transition to adulthood is often neither sufficient, timely nor well-coordinated, and does not ensure fully informed decision by children with disabilities."
18 For example: Deloitte Access Economics (2017) *Review of education for students with disability in Queensland state schools*. Brisbane: Department of Education and Training. http://education.qld.gov.au/schools/disability/docs/

disability-review-report.pdf (retrieved July 3rd 2017 15.04 AEST); Victoria Department of Education and Training (2016) *Review of the program for students with disabilities*. Melbourne: DET. www.education.vic.gov.au/Docu ments/about/department/PSD-Review-Report.pdf (retrieved July 3rd 2017 15.09 AEST). Shaddock, A., Packer, S. & Roy, A. (2015) *Schools for all children and young people: report of the expert panel on students with complex needs and challenging behaviour*. Canberra: Australian Capital Territory Department for Education.

19 Walker, P. (2017) Report sparks concern about how schools support students with disabilities. *The Conversation*. June 13th 12.34 AEST. https://theconver sation.com/report-sparks-concern-about-how-schools-support-students-with-disabilities-78753 (Retrieved July 4th 2017 18.53 AEST).

20 Garner, H. (1993) Killing Daniel. In H. Garner (Ed.) (2017) *The collected short non-fiction: true stories*. Melbourne: The Text Publishing Company, page 190.

21 Helen Garner being quoted by Bernadette Brennan in her magnificent review of Garner's life in and of writing. Brennan, B. (2017) *A writing life: Helen Garner and her work*. Melbourne: The Text Publishing Company, page 175.

Interlude

Pilates

Pilates is my latest battle plan. Not wanting to go gentle, I have decided that Joseph's plan to rehabilitate mere boys wounded on the European battlefields during World War 1 might slow time's winged chariot.

On my way to the Rathdowne Street rooms with Radio National as my preferred background noise, I crawled through the intersection of Elgin Street and Lygon Street.

"What are your five favourite albums, James?" enquired the radio broadcaster of her guest, James Morrison, an iconic Australian musician. I adjusted the volume wondering which other trumpeters the jazz virtuoso would land on. The story unfolded. Forgive me for I will paraphrase; search the RN website, as I have; I couldn't get a transcript. Anyway, stories usually improve as they wander away from their source.

James Morrison demurred and instead of selecting five tracks as he has done before, he opted for one album. He told the story of how as an 11-year-old he first heard Errol Garner's *Concert by the Sea*. He spoke of how the trio comprising Errol Garner (piano), Eddie Calhoun (bass) and Denzel Best (drums) drove to a church hall in Carmel, California, on 19 September 1955 to play an afternoon gig. Not an important gig in prospect. Someone had recorded them on a primitive tape recorder and from that the album was born. For James Morrison, the album captures and communicates the mystery of a live performance where there is some kind of alchemy that connects musicians each to the other as well as the musicians and the audience to each other in a performative communion. The recording resonates that chemistry; that musical congress.

As someone who has fumbled his way through gigs with friends, I have felt occasions where there is that union between musicians and audience, each understanding and delighting in their imperfect achievement in sound. James described that with reference to Errol Garner's Carmel recording. The quality and achievement of the music on that day 62 years ago in that place depended upon a fusion of all of the elements: the virtuosity of the musicians and their sensibility of each other; the readiness, enthusiasm and knowledge of the audience; and the spirit of place. The musicians and audience bring their differences to the venue and respectfully seal a pledge to meld these differences to enact the music.

Finding that unity of purpose within the complex amalgam of elements that constitutes an inclusive school seems to be a rare achievement. How to capture such a performance? Jazz musicians are schooled formally and informally to hone their craft. How to school our educators and a school community for inclusion? How to realise that the differences between the players and the interplay and union of those differences actually constitutes the magic? What would your music teacher or mentor tell you? It may go like this: select the challenging score, practice every day by yourself and regularly with your combo. Talk about the score and your playing. Seek differences to build greater possibility. Record and listen (no, really listen) and push each other to get it right. And make sure that you all retain fun and enjoyment throughout.

1   A time for Frank speaking

Frank Zappa left this world too soon, dying at the age of 52. His musical legacy, comprising some of the most complicated polyrhythms and atonal soundscapes, is immense. He left us much more. Some of his onstage remarks, retorts in interviews and his writing, are now iconic. They are often referenced in work on almost any subject. Let me join that tradition as a way of commencing this essay.

In his autobiography entitled *The Real Frank Zappa* Book,[1] he opens one section with the heading: ***Jazz: The Music of Unemployment***. His relationship with jazz was enigmatic as musicologist Geoff Wills[2] demonstrates with forensic zeal. While Zappa declared his disdain for jazz, in the various incarnations of his bands and orchestras, most notably The Mothers of Invention, he surrounded himself with musicians with stellar jazz pedigrees. A quick and incomplete roll call includes: Bruce, Tom and Walter Fowler, Ruth and Ian Underwood, Gary Barone, Jean Luc Ponty, George Duke, John Guerin, Allan Zavod, Vinnie Colaiuta, Chester Thompson, Chad Wackerman and Jay Migliori. Moreover, his music embraced many genres within the jazz family. How could *Hot Rats* be heard as anything but a highly derivative and delightful achievement in jazz? Listen to the album *Roxy and Elsewhere* and you will hear Zappa tell the audience that: *"Jazz is not dead . . . it just smells funny"*. For devotees of Zappa and of jazz, the quote is amusing yet perplexing.

My take on this quote from Zappa involves two explanations. The first is that he was characteristically prodding the lion of respectability with the broomstick of irreverence. It was just a humorous provocation that he really hadn't thought about too much. Second, and more plausibly, he might be saying that all artistic genres go through a similar cycle: they confront what has gone before, offering up something that is apparently radical, innovative, new. And then, they become respectable and predictable. With age – vitality recedes; the aroma of adrenaline is replaced by the stench of atrophy. I watched an interview on Canadian television with jazz saxophonist Branford Marsalis who spoke of committing Bach's 186 rules of harmony to memory before breaking them. "Whose rules", he asked, "did Bach break when he established the canon?" Today's radical utterances, like yesterday's, morph into tomorrow's conservatism.

John Gennari commences his text on jazz and its critics[3] by declaring that his interest in jazz and the reportage that surrounds it arose *"in the late 1970s (when) word of jazz's death was all around"*. I suspect that Zappa too was responding to the *talk of the time*, but with his own seriously humorous inflection that as *"a cornerstone of modern cultural imagination"*,[4] jazz would again seed the confronting new sounds that would set in train a challenging progressive genre. Some may postulate that this was Zappa's intent.

I am not breaking new ground here. In *Reflections on Exile* Edward Said presents an elegant essay entitled *"Travelling Theory Reconsidered"*[5] wherein he reminds us that by the time Georg Lukas's theory of reification was adopted by Lucien Goldman in Paris and Raymond Williams in Cambridge it had lost its *"original power and rebelliousness"*. Theories born from and organically linked to, historical circumstances are *"degraded and subdued"* by the passage of time and changing circumstances. They become a *"relatively tame academic substitute for the real thing"* whose essential purpose was disruption culminating in political change.

Previously I have registered my view that inclusive education is nearing exhaustion from its extensive global and trans-paradigmatic travels. Contemporary theories of inclusive education, to paraphrase Said, have largely been *tamed and domesticated* – thereby losing their *insurrectionary zeal*. I say *theories* because there is no general theory of inclusive education. It could be described as an assembly hall within which gather disparate and desperate postulations and propositions about the intersections of human and social pathology with education. Almost a decade ago Julie Allan and I described inclusive education as a *"troubled and troubling"* field of education research housing highly charged, often emotive and personalised, contests.[6] Nothing seems to have changed. Or has it? The reluctant acceptance of inclusive education as an organising mantra has not prompted an interrogation of the "essence of exclusion", the smelly side of schooling, or a will to change the fundamental settings that forms and rejuvenates it.

What are our options then? Capitulation? Inclusive education could dig its hands deep into its pockets, lower its head and shuffle off exhausted by attempts to resist the comfortable co-dependence of regular and special education. The near perfect attempt to silence inclusive education through the colonisation of its language and new franchising deals with units and classrooms in the neighbourhood school diminishes inclusive education's original manifesto of justice for children and young people with disabilities.

Retreat will not do. An unobstructed triumph of exclusion is not really an option. Rather than abandon inclusive education and look for the next set of words with which to mount the battle against the exclusion of vulnerable population groups, let us go back to first principles and apply them to the changed and ever-changing circumstances of this *liquid* twenty-first century where commitment is illusory. This is the book's hoarse whisper of hope that may simply be grasping at another opportunity to fail better.[7]

Them bones, them bones

I commenced this book with the proposition that exclusion resides deep in the bones of education; now is the time for explication. This really isn't a hard case to put together. Education, as Connell counselled almost a quarter of a century ago, *"is not simply a mirror of social or cultural inequalities"*. *"That"*, she says, *"is all too still an image. Education systems are busy institutions. They are vibrantly involved in the production of social hierarchies. They select and exclude their own clients; they expand credentialed labour markets; they produce and disseminate particular kinds of knowledge to particular users"*.[8] Connell, like others in what was then called the *New Sociology of Education*,[9] laid down the foundations for ensuing research into the complex relationships and intersections between schooling and social divisions according to class, race, ethnicity, indigeneity, gender, geographic location, sexuality, perceived ability, or disability and religion. To be sure, there have emerged lines of conceptual division surrounding the understanding of the intersections of schooling, the structure of society and a person's agency or control over their experience of education, levels of achievement and points of social transition. Nevertheless, there is ample evidence to suggest that the assignment of failure is structurally, rather than randomly, assigned through the division of schools according to *postcodes* of privilege and disadvantage.[10] In other words the structures and cultures of schooling reinforce privilege and exacerbate disadvantage according to the taut and taught, boundaries of the neo-liberal imagination. Accordingly, there is no shortage of data demonstrating academic underachievement and diminished educational experiences according to students' class, gender, race, ethnicity, or perceived ability or disability.[11]

Inequality, and its fellow traveller, exclusion, are woven so tightly into the fabric of education, it often goes unacknowledged. I will try to avoid the reductionism that goes hand in hand with an attempt to compose a three-paragraph précis of the funding and elaborate structures of education in Australia. Describing Australian education funding to someone from elsewhere invariably evokes looks of puzzlement as we describe the gravity-defying upward redistribution of taxation. People are quite correctly stunned by our fiscal endorsement of educational privilege and disadvantage.

Australia is a Federation of six (6) states (New South Wales, Victoria, Queensland, South Australia, Western Australia and Tasmania) and two (2) territories (the Northern Territory and the Australian Capital Territory). The state and territory governments are predominantly responsible for the financing of what is referred to as the state school sector. Additionally, there is a Roman Catholic system of diocesan-based schools funded by Catholic Education Offices and tuition fees applied to their students' families or caregivers in each state and territory. There are also systemic Roman Catholic schools financed by tuition fees and by teaching orders of the church – for example, the Christian Brothers or the Carmelite Sisters. Alongside these schools is a sector, which is variously referred to as the *independent* or *private school sector*. While parents pay tuition fees and capital levees to these schools, they also receive per capita funding from the Federal government. Federal funds are also transferred to Catholic schools: systemic and orders.

It would be misleading to say that the '*independent*' and the Catholic sectors exclusively represent privilege. There is range within the sectors. The local Catholic parish school in the western suburbs of Melbourne just scrapes by in comparison to a Jesuit School within a brisk walk to Sydney's harbour. A market has emerged for 'affordable' independent schooling. As is the case internationally,[12] state schools are also characterised by a range in privilege and disadvantage according to postcode, and this has direct implications for the curriculum, quality of teaching and opportunities for students.[13] The material resources that a school may draw from its community to support and augment the school programme varies by postcode. It is important to insert a note that many a so-called disadvantaged school capitalises cultural resources from its community to build robust programmes.

Some state schools position themselves as selective academic schools much like the grammar school in England. They present as the public private school. This activity then generates competition to buy into property in the school zone when zones are retained. The attendant gentrification acts as a filter for selection of the suitable children for the school and its all-important *My School website* profile.[14] This form of educational product differentiation is endorsed by jurisdictions where so-called *autonomous status* is granted to schools according to stated criteria. Funding incentives are offered to encourage schools to achieve this status. Readers will recognise a variation on a theme expressed as Charter Schools in the US, Academies in England and Independent and autonomous government schools in Singapore. Maija Salokangas and Mel Ainscow's *Inside the Autonomous School* reveals the proscribed boundaries of the new autonomy.[15] The drive to strike distinctiveness to derive benefit from the increasingly competitive education market may be expressed in curriculum specialisation such as STEM, Sports or Creative Arts or in terms of student identities such as a school for the gifted and talented child or the child with autism. Echoes of the school for the maladjusted or the delicate child become more audible.[16]

Over time there has been a drift from the state schools sector to the independent schools sector fuelled by a belief in the suggested superiority of the education in private schooling and the promise of greater opportunities. The population size of the sectors is presented in Table 1.1 *Australian School Sectors*.

Students are further divided between regular and special schools. This is so entrenched now that it is seen as a natural and proper division rather than an historical artefact and administrative predisposition. Most children, including many children with disabilities, attend their local neighbourhood school along with their siblings and other children from the neighbourhood. A small, but growing, minority of children who have been identified as having special educational needs or disabilities are *placed in* and attend special schools. Chris Boyle from The University of Exeter with colleagues

Table 1.1 Australian School Sectors – Total Student Enrolment in Australian Schools in 2013–6,798,226

State Schools	65.4%
Catholic Schools	20.2%
Independent Schools	14.4%

Source: Australian Bureau of Statistics, 2017

Jo Anderson and Natalie Swayn draw on data from the Australian Bureau of Statistics in an article for *The Conversation* entitled, 'Australia lags behind the evidence on special schools', that charts the increase of schools across Australia between 1999 and 2013 by 3%; in that same period special schools increased by 17%.[17] Table 1.2: *Special and Regular School Attendance* shows a breakdown of attendance in special and regular schools by the Australian state and territory jurisdictions.

Focusing on the data from the Department of Education and Training Victoria (DET) is instructive. Looking at *Table 1.3: DET Victoria – Students with Disabilities in Government Schools*, there is an apparent stability in the data over five years (2012–2016). There has apparently been little variation in enrolments of children with disabilities in special schools, as a percentage of total student population in Victoria between the years 2012 and 2015.

Table 1.2 Special and Regular School Attendance

State/Territory	Students without disabilities	Students with disabilities	Students with disabilities
		Attending Special School	Attending Regular School
New South Wales	7,109,623	12,966	73,910
Victoria	5,546,311	7,994	57,197
Queensland	4,458,232	7,007	53,018
South Australia	1,619,316	1,561	17,403
Western Australia	2,313,972	2,949	29,334
Tasmania	485,051	575	9,156
Northern Territory	143,800	360	829
Australian Capital Territory	361,081	662	4,770

Source: Australian Bureau of Statistics 2012

Table 1.3 DET Victoria – Students with Disabilities in Government Schools (FTE)

YEAR	In Regular Schools	In Special Schools	Total	% Of Total Student Cohort
2012	11,875	9,721	21,596	4.0
2013	12,034	10,247	22,281	4.0
2014	12,218	10,704	22,922	4.1
2015	12,671	11,264	23,936	4.2
2016	12,980	11,515	24,495	4.2

Source: DET Victoria, April 2017, www.education.vic.gov.au/Documents/about/department/brochureapril2017.pdf (Retrieved: July 7th 13:51 AEST)

Indeed, after two years of no change, the number of students with disabilities in special schools incrementally climbs by 0.2%. Although the ratios may vary between jurisdictions nationally and internationally, the apparent stability of enrolments of children in special schools remains. Data, as Dan Levitin counsels, is not always what it seems.[18] The more data, he says, that we put into a table, the less interpretable it becomes and the more difficult it is for most people to be able to detect patterns or recognise trends. So, we often settle on representations that give us but a fraction of the story. Think then, of the implications of this for evidence-driven policymaking. Or, is it policy-driven evidence making?

Is there a story within, outside of or behind the tables in this essay? What are those more complete stories? Let's arm ourselves with some extraneous questions to unsettle our reading of Table 1.3. First, we might ask the rudimentary questions and then pursue the interrogation further with '*ruder*mentary' enquiries.

Some rudimentary questions:

What happens to this table when we start to disaggregate the data (both for students with disabilities in regular schools and for students with disabilities in special schools)?

Who are we talking about and are they stable population cohorts?

What does the data look like at different stages of schooling?

Are there other factors that may affect the data that demands elaboration of the table (gender, ethnicity, geographic location, socio-economic status)?

Are there country-specific factors that would alter the data significantly?

Some "*ruder*mentary" questions:

What is the purpose of the table?

Who decided on the data to be gathered?

Who determined the form of presentation?

What was excluded from the data set?

With this larger bag of questions my interrogation of Table 1.3 might look like this:

How is it decided that you are a student with a disability in Victoria? What do prevalence rates look like over time across and within localities? Are there differences between and within urban and rural schools? Are there differences that can be detected between different regions within a jurisdiction? Are there intersections that appear significant such as gender, class, culture, or ethnic identity?

Do students with disabilities start their schooling at a special school or regular school and stay in that setting for the duration of their schooling? Is the flow of students in both directions (as if! . . . and here we speak not of that curious act of benevolence called reverse integration)? Have there been changes in population characteristics in both places or either place over time?

Are there categories of disability where prevalence is greater or smaller in either school setting (regular or special)? What are the reasons for this?

Can we detect demand and/or supply side changes over time, and what does this signify?

Are there changes in education policies, programmes or funding that impact either or both school settings?

What is happening to the organisation in regular schools and special schools over time that may impact data?

More careful and extensive interrogation yields richer data sets. Accordingly, we will see the growth of private special and alternative schools that contribute to the stability of the picture presented in Table 1.3. There may also be data to suggest that segregation is now occurring within the regular school. What does the home-schooling data look like – does it tell us anything about students with disability and their schooling?

Why would it be otherwise?

Let's not feign surprise. The mobilisation of exclusion through the structures, processes, programmes and ethos; that is, the cultures, of schooling is an embodiment of our social condition. Neoliberalism provides an ethical framework for the organisation and operation of our social institutions including schooling. Schools are forged within the furnace of competitive individualism, and students are reduced to the bearers of results. They become individually measurable units that when aggregated reveal the performance of a teacher, a school, a school district, state jurisdiction or nation-state. As individual units, students manifest risk or opportunity.

Having embraced, and what a passionate entanglement it is, the conjecture of Hayek and Friedman, neoliberalism maintains that disparities will be corrected by an unencumbered marketplace. There will be, maintain the proponents of this credo, a trickle-down of wealth to smooth inevitable or natural inequities. This proposition is worth testing, if only in a cursory manner here.

Trickle-down or waterboarding?

Poverty is not just a north/south phenomenon. It walks with us – it stalks us – however much we hope that erecting walls and installing CCTV around our housing developments will remove its constant reminder of and embarrassment to our privilege. Establishing the fact of inequality is not challenging. By utilising the work of economists and geographers we may apply the demographic brushstrokes within which we can insert the personal dimensions of global and local immiseration.

Economists such as Sachs, Picketty, Atkinson, Varoufakis and Milanovic collectively chart the movement of capital and corresponding patterns of inequity.[19] Thomas Picketty, for example, analyses shifts in the concentration and structure of wealth over time:

> *The overall importance of capital today, as noted, is not very different from what it was in the eighteenth century. Only its form has changed: capital was once mainly land but is now industrial, financial and real estate. We also know that the concentration of wealth remains high, although it is noticeably less extreme than it was a century ago. The poorest half of the population still owns nothing, but there is now a patrimonial middle class that owns between a quarter and a third of total wealth, and the wealthiest 10 per cent now own only two-thirds of what there is to own rather than nine-tenths.*[20]

Professor Anthony Atkinson from the UK examines income inequalities in the US and the UK to reflect income inequality between the top 1 per cent of the population and the rest. He, like others,[21] tracks a steady increase in the income gap.

> *Today, the share of the top 1 per cent has returned to the value of 100 years ago. The top 1 per cent in the US now receives close to one-fifth of total gross income – meaning that, on average, they have twenty times their proportionate share. Within the top 1 per cent, too, there is considerable inequality: the share of the top 1 per cent of those within the top 1 per cent (that is, the top 0.01 per cent) is also around one-fifth*

of the total income of this group. This means that 1/10,000 of the population receives 1/25 of the total income.[22]

He goes on to suggest that comparing the US distribution of income with that of the UK is almost akin to replacing the 'S' with the 'K'.

The share of the top 1 per cent in the UK is lower than that in the US, but this group still receives one-eighth of total gross income.[23]

Wilkinson and Pickett, Stiglitz, Bauman and Dorling collectively advance a persuasive account of the deleterious impacts of inequality and economic injustice.[24] Indeed, Wilkinson and Pickett demonstrate that the greater the inequality gap is in affluent countries, the more dysfunctional they become. This dysfunction is reflected in data showing escalations of incarceration, welfare support reliance, poor health and educational underachievement. Geographers such as Harvey, Sibley and Dorling[25] provide the fine detail of the human costs of *geographies of difference* that resonate with Kozol's[26] earlier descriptions of *death zones* in American cities that reflect deep divisions of wealth according to race.

Data has a tendency to obscure the human face of social division and exclusion. Exclusion is described in technical, apparently objective, language to remove human complicity in rendering people *useless* to the economy and subject to the unremitting struggle of a life in poverty. In Bauman's words, we are seduced by the technical explanations of the causes of deep social divisions:

> . . . *the production of human waste has all the markings of an impersonal, purely technical issue. The principal actors in the drama are 'terms of trade', 'market demands', 'competitive pressures', 'productivity' or 'efficiency requirements', all covering up or explicitly denying any connection with the intentions, will, decisions and actions of real humans with names and addresses.*[27]

In 2012 *The Briefing* column of *The Economist* personalises the individual costs of poverty in America.[28] The protagonist in the story is Emma Hamilton. She is a loader in a factory in Sumter, South Carolina. Emma's hand was crushed in an industrial accident at the factory she had worked at for seven years. Unable to work, Emma lost her house. She collects cans for change during the daytime. At night, she sleeps in her van with her son in a shopping centre car park. Coincidentally, Emma receives treatment for chronic pain in her leg from a medical assistant called Patricia Dunham. Patricia holds down two jobs, one at the medical clinic, the second at a restaurant.

Her minimum-wage salary supports her infirm husband, buying expensive medications for him and also for their son who has a behaviour disorder. Chronic illness and a record of incarceration prevent her husband's re-entry to the labour market. Her work gives no access to medical insurance and she is paying off her mother's funeral expenses. Falling behind in car loan repayments, it was repossessed and she makes the long and unsafe journey to work at night on foot and by public transport. If her work were regular, her salary would amount to $32,135.70 a year before taxation deductions. This is below the poverty line. According to *The Economist* 15 per cent of Americans, some 46.2 million people, live below the poverty line and are in need of assistance. Inequality describes suffering human faces rendered less visceral by the data. Those faces are becoming all too real as the drive for deportation of illegal workers escalates. One could speculate about the fate of the American economy should it lose this source of underpaid labour. Whither the self-correcting market?

Wherever our finger lands on the spinning globe, the more or less acute divisions shuffle forward. While working in Ethiopia recently in the comfort of a hotel conference room in Addis Ababa, people who had travelled for days on tired and battered buses across scared and crumbling roadways described the grip of the present drought. It is a drought now worse than in the 1980s when the world was mobilised by Sir Bob Geldof's images of children quietly dying from the ravages of severe malnutrition and treatable diseases that prey on bodies already depleted by poverty. Like their wells, the trickle-down of wealth has dried up. Those who perish become even more invisible than that invisible hand of economic equilibrium.

Bauman[29] and Sennett[30] describe how changes in the structure of work and the labour market enforce people to live under the *"spectre of useless"*. Feared redundancy drives a competitive wedge through the heart of communities. People scramble against and over each other to stave off economic uselessness. Inevitably there are *collateral casualties* of the contraction or relocation of the labour market that generates "surplus populations". These people are in Bauman's terms the *human waste* of liquid modernity. Paradoxically, despite intensifying competition, the dominant political discourse is framed in the language of inclusion, multiculturalism and communitarianism. The reality, observes Bauman, is the growing fear of the stranger, and each society will create its own set of strangers in its own inimitable way.[31] Ours is an age, he says, of mixaphobia.[32]

Can we not recognise this scenario being played out in and through schools? Schools are pressed to compete with each other to build a profile of academic success. Their results are aggregated so that countries compete with each other to scramble up performance league tables. Students are the schools' assets and risks. Minimising risk through early detection, containment or elimination is established as an operating rationale and practice.

Does this smell funny to you, Frank?

The Department of Education and Training in Queensland has annual show-case awards for educational excellence. This is not in itself remarkable; it is done in many other jurisdictions. Neither is it remarkable that there are categories of awards in order to be able to showcase different areas of excellence of educational activity and honour the achievement of a larger number of schools. There should be a celebration of the achievements of public education; the popular media isn't much interested. The categories are sponsored by various external organisations. Accordingly, there is the *Village Roadshow Theme Parks Award for Excellence in Inclusive Education*. For this observer, it is remarkable that the recipient of last year's award was Mt Omaney Special School. Indeed, there were two other special schools that were regional finalists in the *Village Roadshow Theme Parks Award for Excellence in Inclusive Education*. Is this not the now complete appropriation of inclusive education? At the very least, it represents what Edward Said describes as the "taming and domestication" of a once rebellious and insurrectionary movement. Are your olfactory sensibilities not affronted?

How did it come to this?

The roll-off-the-tongue couplets *inclusive education* and *inclusive schooling* are now as established in the education lexicon as is the phrase *special educational needs*. In fact, the coupling and conflation of these three terms of reference is commonplace. Postgraduate programmes are offered at universities around the world in *special needs and inclusive education*. Or, if you prefer, *inclusive and special needs education*. Education jurisdictions develop and distribute policies under the heading of 'inclusive education and special educational needs'. Publishing houses also use this tag to catalogue their imprint titles. This is of course a reflection of the key search words that are most frequently used by authors needing to increase their citations and research impact statements. From its initial declaration of a critique of special education, much has changed.[33] Users are apparently unaware of the paradox they propagate.[34]

For those of us who want to look at numbers, we can see in Table 1.4: *Selected Search Engine Data* that there is no shortage of links to "inclusive education" and "inclusive schooling". Remembering Daniel Levitin's counsel about crude tables such as this, I acknowledge that these data are not disaggregated at all. They do not reflect the type of entry being counted, its origin or its quality. This is a representation of activity to demonstrate

Table 1.4 Selected Search Engine Data

Search subject	Google	Google Scholar	Bing	Refseek
Inclusive education	15,100,000 (0.48 seconds)	3,080,000 (0.03 seconds)	8,400,000	50,500,000 (0.37 seconds)
Inclusive schooling	1,030,000 (0.39 seconds)	232,000 (0.09 seconds)	138,000,000	911,000 (0.41 seconds)

the volume of references to inclusive education and inclusive schooling – nothing more.

Adequately, explaining this rapid transformation of a theory and attendant practices would require a more searching analysis than I am about to offer. For the purposes of this essay I will propose three lines of enquiry or themes as a beginning for your further consideration.

1 Global education movements

The *Programme for International Student Assessment* now familiar as its acronym **PISA**, *Trends in International Maths and Science Study* – **TIMSS**, and the *Progress in International Reading Literacy Study* – **PIRLS** have been established as global benchmarks for assessing the performance of national education systems. An international league-table has been established, and education policymakers either nervously or confidently await the next iteration. This is FIFA World Cup for education policymakers. This is a monumental development in the international education landscape over the past 15 years.

These high-stakes assessment programmes reach across and deep into nations to shape education policies, curriculum and thinking. For instance, Australia has fashioned its own facsimile. The *National Assessment Program – Literacy and Numeracy* (NAPLAN) was developed on behalf of the Council of Australian Governments (COAG) to chart and improve the performance of students across Australia in maths and literacy. NAPLAN, like other testing programmes,[35] has its supporters and detractors. Some argue that it allows us to track school and jurisdiction performance over time. Others say its scope is too narrow and forces a dangerous contraction of the curriculum priorities; that it encourages test training and promotes anxiety amongst students and teachers.

Supra-organisations such as, and not limited to, the Organisation of Economic Cooperation and Development (OECD), United Nations Educational, Scientific and Cultural Organisation (UNESCO), United Nations Children's Fund (UNICEF), the World Bank, the International Monetary Fund (IMF), the Bill and Melinda Gates Foundation, the George Soros Open Society

Foundations, Pearson, and Cambridge International Examinations converge to shape global education policy and practice. They defy national boundaries or other demarcations described as countries of the north and countries of the south as major influencers of education policy.

Some of these organisations such as UNESCO, UNICEF, the OECD and the World Bank have also shaped the rapid global growth and popularisation of inclusive education and have sought, more or less, to distinguish it from traditional special education or segregated schooling. This proposition is debatable as many within these organisations argue from the standpoint of their special education training.

The origins of this internationalisation of inclusive education is typically linked to the World Education Forums of Jomtien in Thailand in 1990 and more frequently to Salamanca in Spain in 1994 under the banner of *Education for All*.[36] *Education for All* referred to increasing access, presence, participation and success for all children. In its sights were the barriers that restricted the participation of the girl child, of children living in extreme poverty, children with disabilities, children displaced or excluded from school by conflict, traveller children across Europe, children excluded by racism, by their sexuality, or by tribal, ethnic and religious affiliations, and children in remote locations. You can see that there was a strong development agenda, but of course we know that exclusion walks amongst us; it casts a permanent shadow over our privilege, some elements of the agenda were as relevant to those in countries of the north as the south. Advocates for children with disabilities applied *education for all* as a rallying call for their inclusion in the neighbourhood school and the dismantling of segregation.

The 1994 *Salamanca Statement and Framework for Action on Special Needs Education* is typically held up as the high-water mark for progressing inclusive education for students with disabilities.[37] The delegates proposed that inclusive education means that:

> . . . *schools should accommodate all children regardless of their physical, intellectual, social, emotional, linguistic or other conditions. This should include disabled and gifted children, street and working children, children from remote or nomadic populations, children from linguistic, ethnic or cultural minorities and children from other disadvantaged or marginalised areas or groups.*[38]

Two of the principles contained within the Salamanca Statement and endorsed by 92 governments are worth noting here:

- *Those with special educational needs must have access to regular schools which will accommodate them within a child-centred pedagogy capable of meeting these needs;*

- *Regular schools with this inclusive orientation are the most effective means of combating discriminatory attitudes, creating welcoming communities, building an inclusive society and achieving education for all; moreover, they provide an effective education to the majority of children and improve the efficiency and ultimately the cost effectiveness of the entire system.*[39]

There it is reader – "special educational needs". Who would have predicted the traction and grip of Warnock's terminology?

2 Human rights and anti-discrimination legislation

Responding to litigation and the groundswell of civil-rights movements for the elimination of discrimination against people on the basis of race, gender, disability and sexuality, we have witnessed the establishment of anti-discrimination legislation to protect the ordinary rights of citizens in diverse communities in countries around the world. Concurrently, the United Nations has struck international conventions to promote and protect the rights of people subject to discrimination and to safeguard children. Examples of this are the *United Nations Convention on the Rights of the Child*[40] and the *United Nations Convention on the Rights of Persons with Disabilities and Optional Protocol* (2006). In 2017 174 Ratifications of the United Nations Convention on the Rights of Persons with Disabilities (UNCRPD) have been struck and 92 ratifications of the Optional Protocol.[41] *Article 24: Education* directs signatories of UNCRPD to provide access to an inclusive education for persons with disabilities. Writing in 2016 the United Nations Committee on the Rights of Persons with Disabilities makes clear their conceptualisation of inclusive education:

> *The Committee highlights the importance of recognising the differences between exclusion, segregation, integration and inclusion. Exclusion occurs when students are directly or indirectly prevented from or denied access to education in any form. Segregation occurs when the education of students with disabilities is provided in separate environments designed or used to respond to a particular or various impairments, in isolation from students without disabilities. Integration is a process of placing persons with disabilities in existing mainstream educational institutions, as long as the former can adjust to the standardized requirements of such institutions.*[42] *Inclusion involves a process of systemic reform embodying changes and modifications in content, teaching methods, approaches, structures and strategies in education to overcome barriers with a vision serving to provide all students of the relevant age range with an equitable and participatory*

learning experience and environment that best corresponds to their requirements and preferences. Placing students with disabilities within mainstream classes without accompanying structural changes to, for example, organisation, curriculum and teaching and learning strategies, does not constitute inclusion.

At the risk of diversion, it may be worth considering extracts from the observers' reports on the progress of three countries in their implementation of UNCRPD Article 24. The 2013 UNCRPD Committee Report on Australia state:

> *"The Committee is concerned that despite the Disability Standards for Education established to ensure access to education on an equal basis, students with disabilities continue to be placed in special schools and many of those who are in regular schools are largely confined to special classes or units. The Committee is further concerned that students with disabilities enrolled in regular schools receive a substandard education due to lack of reasonable accommodation. The Committee is also concerned that secondary school completion rates for students with disabilities are about half of those for people without disability".*

The 2014 New Zealand UNCRPD observers' report states:

> *"The Committee notes the steps being taken to increase inclusive primary and secondary education, and the ongoing challenges to making the education system fully inclusive, such as the lack of reasonable accommodation. The Committee is concerned at reports indicating that children with disabilities experience bullying in schools, and notes that there is no enforceable right to inclusive education".*

The 2016 UK UNCRC Committee Report states:

(*a*) *Many children with disabilities do not see that their views are given due weight in making personal decisions in their life, including choice of support and future;*

(*b*) *Many children with disabilities are still placed in special schools or special units in mainstream schools and many school buildings and facilities are not made fully accessible to children with disabilities;*

(*c*) *Provision of the support for transition to adulthood is often neither sufficient, timely nor well-coordinated, and does not ensure fully informed decision by children with disabilities.*

These statements from the UNCRD observers are stark and unsurprising. Such is the cultural grip of special education, it has proven impossible to shake free from its epistemological manacles.

In many jurisdictions around the world, national legislative and regulatory frameworks to prevent discrimination against people with disabilities predated the United Nations Convention on the Rights of Persons with Disabilities. Examples of this include:

- The Americans with Disabilities Act (ADA) 1990 and the Americans with Disabilities Act Amendments Act of 2008. Public Law 94–142 the Education for All Handicapped Children Act (1975) was replaced by the Individuals with Disabilities Education Act (IDEA) in 1990. As part of the No Child Left Behind programme, IDEA was amended and replaced in 2004 by Public Law 108–446 the Individuals with Disabilities Education Improvement Act.[43]
- The Disability Discrimination Act (DDA) – 1992 in Australia provided for the development of the Disability Standards for Education – 2005 which set the obligations and requirements for the education of students with disabilities. The implementation of the Disability Standards for Education has been reviewed (June 2012) and the latest report card for the state and territory education departments shows considerable work to be done to meet these standards.[44]

These are just two examples of legislative frameworks for protection against the discrimination against children with disabilities in education. Such legislation does not guarantee an inclusive education system. Indeed, caveats within legislation such as "least restrictive environment" or "reasonable accommodation" create yawning interpretive chasms into which many children with disabilities; their families and advocates, fall. The point here is to suggest that because of the advancement of anti-discrimination law and the promotion within that of notions of inclusive education, its global uptake, and reinterpretation, has been rapid. Special educators have felt the chill winds of change and have adopted the language of inclusion to explain and defend their professional practice.[45]

3 The resilience of special education

The fusion of ableism, institutional stasis and professional interest has cruelled the fledgling radicalism of special education. The exclusion of students with disabilities from the local school under the presumption that they were uneducable has been a long-standing tradition in education. A hand full of physicians, educators, families and their advocates in different places and times rejected that view. Consequently, they established instructional programmes outside of the regular provision of schooling and took charge of the learning of children with disabilities. This can be described as a radical rejection of the common sense of the time. Exemplifying this, in exquisite prose, Scot Danforth writes of the clandestine teaching of a 10-year-old boy in the Oak Forrest Institution for Delinquent Children by Samuel Kirk "under a small corridor light, so as not to be caught by the staff nurses".[46] Samuel Kirk is seen as one of the founding fathers of special education in North America.

Rather than rehearse a history of special education by chronicling the work of pioneers such as the French and Swiss physicians Jean Marc Gaspard Itard and Johan Jacob Guggenbuhl and many others, it may be acceptable to say that early educational advances for the so-called *feeble-minded* and *crippled child*, for the blind and the deaf child, represented a rejection of the view of the child with disabilities as uneducable. Interventions were conducted outside of regular school systems because these children were excluded. Schooling for children with disabilities was conducted in separate or segregated schools so as to maintain the separation of those children considered normal and those who were not. This demarcation was not simply the preference of what we describe as the regular school system, it was also a belief amongst many people working in segregated schools that children with disabilities should be isolated for the protection and safety of the "*normal*" child. This view was undergirded and elaborated by the growing "science" of eugenics. Stephen Ball examines "the enormously influential work" of Cyril Burt in his 1937 book, *The Backward Child*[47] and his claim to be able to distinguish the "sub-normal child" from the "backward child", the "mentally defective child" from the "backward child". "*His psychological classification*", writes Ball, "*is nothing but a means to an end, a practical aid rather than an indisputable point of scientific diagnosis. The end is management and discipline*".[48]

Once again history defies neat narrative. Special education has not been an uncomplicated and continuous force of educational liberation for children with disabilities. Educating children with disabilities was accepted as being in their best interest and this view, a form of *benevolent humanitarianism*,[49] has prevailed. It has certainly served some people's interests. Separating the education of children with disabilities allowed the regular school to avoid the difficulties of redesigning purpose, plant, programmes, pedagogy and personnel.

The professional knowledge of special education was similarly fenced off to protect professional interest.[50] Special education constitutes a major public investment of finance, infrastructure and human resources on the one hand and belief and emotion on the other. First is the fiscal investment in the provision of infrastructure, programmes and personnel to service special schools and the special needs students who, these days, are a little more dispersed. Second is the investment by the special education workforce in their professional authority, provenance and sustainability. This workforce has grown exponentially over time. They have established professional training, accreditation and regulation and boast large and powerful associations with their journals, conferences and professional development activities. Third is the emotional investment of parents in finding what they see as safe and educationally productive environments for their children who aren't unconditionally welcomed in the neighbourhood school and for whom they quite rightfully feel protective.

University departments of special education have been around for many years, and the expansive field boasts strands that are predominantly organised around children's diagnostic categories. The areas of specialisation within these broader diagnostic categories are continually being elaborated. Billions of dollars are tied up in research institutes and undergraduate and postgraduate teaching programmes. There is a great deal to protect.

Unsurprisingly, there have been full-frontal attacks on inclusive education and disability studies in education researchers from traditional special education researchers like James Kauffman, Gary Sasso and Daniel Hallahan in the US.[51] There have been strident attacks on inclusive education and celebrations of special schools by psychologists such as Michael Farrell in England.[52] In her pamphlet entitled "Special Educational Needs: A New Look", Dame Mary Warnock who was the lead author of the influential 1978 report *Special Educational Needs*, declares that " . . . *even if inclusion is an ideal for society in general, it may not always be an ideal for school*". The "*successful special school seems to be a model that could be followed by others*", she continues.[53] As Mel Ainscow suggests in response to Warnock's pamphlet, her reconsideration has been helpful in moving the issues closer to the centre of the consideration of the on-going nature of education, " . . . *but it has also had a negative impact, in the sense that it has tended to encourage some in the field to retreat into traditional stances*".[54] More astute tacticians have sought to expand their sphere of influence by adopting the more fashionable language of diversity and inclusion and attaching their shingle on the gates of both the special school and the regular school. Special school trophy shelves, notoriously bare affairs, now boast awards for inclusion.

Special education also caught the wave of what Ludwick Fleck[55] calls *thought collectives* around medical and mental health identities. The drift towards describing and then diagnosing disruptive student behaviour, inattention, defiance and truancy as problems of the mind and genetic structure of the student presented school psychologists and special educators with an authority boost. Reference to the *Diagnostic and Statistical Manual of Mental Disorders (DSM)* by school personnel increased and is now commonplace.[56] Available in 18 languages and in print and electronic versions as well as an '*App*' to be bought from the I-tunes shop, *DSM-5* is often referred to through social and popular media as people try to realise greater understanding of themselves and their families. The attribution of disorders is commonplace. Subsequent online networking of the disordered and the proliferation of self-help groups seeking professional help is also well established. The management of the funding models for inclusion across education jurisdictions quickly became the business of school psychologists and special educators since these were the acknowledged experts on disability. DSM and the appropriation of everyday life by psychiatry is a powerful regulator of diverse populations. Michel Foucault's descriptions of the ways in which populations seek to normalise and govern themselves loom large in twenty-first-century education.

A complicated history is not best served by seven short paragraphs. This is simply offered as the pencil markings on a canvas awaiting the finer detail of brush strokes and shades of colour. It is a provocation to test the depth of change present in that which self-describes as inclusive education. It is important that I state for the record that I am not saying that children are not learning in special schools or that they are unhappy. What I am saying is that there are questions based on long-standing evidence of reduced expectations, the racialization of special education and inferior transitions into post-secondary education, training and work for students with disabilities educated in separate special schools. The principle of segregation on the basis of disability is antithetical to the aspirations of an education in and for democracy.

Yes, Frank, it smells funny to me – but who is laughing?

There is much to be despondent about. The language of inclusion has been thoroughly appropriated.[57] The daily activity of exclusion is described as inclusion. Educators will walk you to the nether regions of their school and, grinning with genuine pride, extend an arm to guide you over the threshold of *The Inclusion Room* or *The Inclusion Program*. Therein are gathered children with a range of what are described as disabilities or disorders. Close by is their inclusion teacher (sic. their special teacher) and perhaps an inclusion aide. Alternatively, you may be taken off-campus and whisked away to the freestanding inclusion unit or centre. You may meet with the Chair of the local or provincial Chapter of the Special Education Association or the Executive Committee of the Special School Principals' Association and they will explain why they are the custodians of inclusive education. Whenever this happens, and believe me – happen it does – my nose twitches.

There are other sides to the coin where schools commence from the conviction that all children can learn and be taught. They embrace the principle that all children belong in their local school with their brothers, sisters and neighbours. And by *all,* they really do mean *all.* The child who can't see, the child whose family has been displaced by war and don't speak the school's home language, the child who has difficulty with mobility, the child who doesn't hear, the child whose behaviour is very different or difficult, the child who will be absent for periods of time because of chronic illness or is from an itinerant family, or the child who can't communicate in the way that most other children do. This is an abbreviated list for *all* children. These schools have an idealistic ethos built upon notions of democracy and justice – for which inclusion is a precondition.[58] It seems they have hung on to and are resurrecting the notion of community. If our schools aren't idealistic we are doomed. Public education, as Mike Rose tells us, is our boldest democratic experiment and we are presently "in danger of losing our civic imagination".[59] These schools are innovative, creative and flexible in the way they think about space, programmes and teaching. They offer what Tony Knight described as an *apprenticeship in democracy.*[60]

In his book *The Blind Advantage: How Going Blind Made Me a Stronger Principal and How Including Children with Disabilities Made Our School Better for Everyone*, Bill Henderson[61] tells a story that will be familiar to some and strange to others. The story of O'Hearn Elementary School in Boston is a 20-year tale of including students with disability and, as a result, the attendant improvement of education for all students at O'Hearn Elementary. Staying in Boston, Thomas Hehir describes the properties of an inclusive school with reference to real schools rather than conjecture based upon aspiration. He also extracts and records lessons for schools by describing the journeys of students with disabilities to successfully complete degree programmes at Harvard.[62] Recently, I spent a day in the WISH school in Los Angeles where they too have decided that the purpose of education cannot be reduced to test scores. In a relaxed lunchtime conversation with the heads of the school campuses and a *"specialist support teacher",* I asked them if they could see a time when they could let go of the vernacular of special education which jars with their inclusive ethos and practices that enables children with disabilities to simply be part of the pack. It had not occurred to them as an issue. It is.

You don't have to travel to Massachusetts, enrol in Harvard or venture into the Howard Hughes workers' dormitory suburbs of Los Angeles. There are schools not far from you live where the air is becoming sweet with the scent of inclusion, but at the moment, if what parents keep telling me is correct, you have to hunt for these schools. A word of advice – hold your nose when you go hunting.

Notes

1 Zappa, F. and Occhiogrosso, P. (1990) *The real Frank Zappa book*. London: Picador.
2 Wills, G. (2015) *Zappa and Jazz: did it really smell funny frank?* Kibworth Beauchamp: Matador.
3 Gennari, J. (2016) *Blowin' hot and cool: Jazz and its critics*. Chicago: University of Chicago Press, page 2.
4 Ibid., page 4.
5 Said, E. W. (2000) Travelling theory reconsidered. In E. W. Said (Ed.) *Reflections on exile and other literary and cultural essays*. London: Granta Publications, pages 436–452.
6 Allan, J. and Slee, R. (2008) *Doing inclusive education research*. Rotterdam: Sense Publishers. I had previously used that phrase to describe my father in his eulogy.
7 Beckett, S. (2015) *Waiting for Godot*. London: Faber and Faber; Zizek, S. (2008) *In defense of lost causes*. London: Verso.
8 Connell, R. (1993) *Schools and social justice*. Philadelphia: Temple University Press, page 27.
9 Let me apologise in advance to those I omit from this list of New Sociology of Education researchers, but I am referring to researchers who charted our fledgling understandings of the reproduction of class divisions through the structures, programmes and processes of schooling. In North America, we could refer to work such as Samuel Bowles and Herbert Gintis (1976) *Schooling in capitalist America*. New York: Basic Books; and Michael Apple (1979) *Ideology and curriculum*. London: Routledge and Kegan Paul. In the United Kingdom, the New Sociology of Education was led by and not limited to researchers such as Basil Bernstein (1975) *Class, codes and control; towards a theory of educational transmission* (volumes 1–3). London: Routledge and Kegan Paul; Michael Young (1971) *Knowledge and control*. London: Collier Macmillan; Paul Willis (1977) *Learning to labour*. Farnborough: Saxon House; Michael Young and Geoff Whitty (1977) *Society, state & schooling*. Lewes: Falmer Press; Geoff Whitty (1985) *Sociology and school knowledge: curriculum, theory, research & politics*. London: Methuen & Company. In Australia and New Zealand, Raewyn Connell, Dean Ashenden, Sandra Kessler and Gary Dowsett (1982) *Making the difference: schools, families and social division*. North Sydney: Allen & Unwin; Richard Bates (1978) The new sociology of education: directions for theory and research. *New Zealand Journal of Educational Studies*, 13(1): 3–22. In France, Pierre Bourdieu and Jean-Claude Passeron published their landmark text on cultural reproduction in 1971, Reproduction in Education, Social and Cultural, Paris, Editions de Minuit. The importance and influence of this body of work cannot be overstated. Since there has been a constancy in the reworking of our understandings of the complexity of the relationships and intersections between education, politics and economy.
10 See Richard Teese and John Polesel (1999) *Undemocratic schooling*. Carlton: Melbourne University Press; and Richard Teese (2013) *Academic success and social power: examinations and social power* (Second Edition). North Melbourne: Australian Scholarly Press.
11 See for example Andreas Schleicher (2014) *Equity, excellence and inclusiveness: policy lessons from around the world*. Paris: OECD Publishing. OECD

(2012) *Equity and quality in education: supporting disadvantaged students and schools*. Paris: OECD Publishing. Researchers such as Danny Dorling (2015) *Injustice: why social inequalities persist*; and Richard Wilkinson and Kate Pickett (2010) *The spirit level: why equality is better for everyone*. London: Penguin whose work is dedicated to mapping injustice and inequality, also chart the contribution of education to the perpetuation of privilege and disadvantage. See also Danny Dorling (2017) *The equality effect: improving life for everyone*. Oxford: New Internationalist Publications.

12 Ball, S. J. (2012) *Global education inc.: new policy networks and the neoliberal imaginary*. Abingdon: Routledge.

13 See Op. Cit. Richard Teese (2013).

14 The My School website is published by the Australian Curriculum, Assessment and Reporting Authority (www.myschool.edu.au) to provide parents and communities with information compiled by schools about their profile and performance in comparison with other schools with like student cohorts.

15 Salokangas, M. and Ainscow, M. (2018) *Inside the autonomous school: making sense of a global educational trend*. Abingdon: Routledge.

16 See Sally Tomlinson's table of Statutory Categories of Handicap 1886–1981, page 61, *A sociology of special education*, London: Routledge and Kegan Paul, 1982.

17 Boyle, C., Anderson, J. and Swayn, N. (2015) Australia lags behind the evidence on special schools. *The Conversation*. August 5th 05.35 AEST. https://thecon versation.com/australia-lags-behind-the-evidence-on-special-schools-41343 (Retrieved 7th July 2017 13.55 AEST).

18 Levitin, D. (2016) *A field guide to lies and statistics*. New York: Viking an imprint of Penguin Books.

19 Atkinson, A. B. (2015) *Inequality: what can be done?* Cambridge: Harvard University Press. Milanović, B. (2016) *Global inequality: a new approach for the age of globalization*. Cambridge, MA: The Belknap Press of Harvard University Press. Piketty, T. (2014) *Capital in the twenty-first century*. Cambridge, MA: The Belknap Press of Harvard University Press. Sachs, J. (2012) *The price of civilization*. London: Vintage. Sachs, J. (2006) *The end of poverty: economic possibilities for our time*. New York: Penguin Books. Varoufakis, Y. (2016) *And the weak suffer what they must?* London: The Bodley Head.

20 Op. cit. (Picketty, 2014): 377.

21 Op. cit. (Wilkinson & Pickett, 2010).

22 Op. cit. (Atkinson, 2015): 19–20.

23 Ibid., page 20.

24 Wilkinson, R. G. and Pickett, K. (2010) *The spirit level: why equality is better for everyone*. London: Penguin. Stiglitz, J. E. (2012) *The price of inequality: how today's divided society endangers our future*. New York: W.W. Norton & Co. Bauman, Z. (2013) *Does the richness of the few benefit us all?* Cambridge: Polity. Dorling, D. (2014) *Inequality and the 1%*. London: Verso.

25 Sibley, D. (1995) *Geographies of exclusion: society and difference in the West*. London: Routledge; Harvey, D. (1996) *Justice, nature, and the geography of difference*. Cambridge, MA: Blackwell Publishers; Dorling, D. (2013) *The 32 stops: the central line*. London: Penguin.

26 Kozol, J. (1991) *Savage inequalities: children in America's schools*. New York: Crown Publishers.

27 Op. cit. (Bauman, 2004): 40.

28 The Economist (2012) *Briefings: in need of help*, November 10–16, pages 23–25.
29 Bauman, Z. (2004) *Wasted lives: modernity and its outcasts*. Cambridge: Polity.
30 Sennett, R. (2006) *The culture of the new capitalism*. New Haven: Yale University.
31 Bauman, Z. (1997) *Postmodernity and its discontents*. Cambridge: Polity.
32 Bauman, Z. (2013) *Does the richness of the few benefit us all?* Cambridge: Polity. Bauman, Z. (2008) *Does ethics have a chance in a world of consumers?* Cambridge, MA: Harvard University Press.
33 Slee, R. (2011) *The irregular school*. Abingdon: Routledge.
34 Walton, E. L. (2016) *The language of inclusive education: exploring speaking, listening, reading, and writing*. Abingdon: Routledge.
35 See Stobart, G. (2008) *Testing times: the uses and abuses of assessment*. London: Routledge; Sacks, P. (1999) *Standardized minds: the high price of America's testing culture and what we can do to change it*. Cambridge, MA: Perseus Books; Ravitch, D. (2011) *The death and life of the great American school system: how testing and choice are undermining education*. New York: Basic Books; Meyer, H. and Benavot, A. (2013) *PISA, power & policy: the emergence of global educational governance*. Didcot: Symposium Books.
36 UNESCO (1994) *The Salamanca world conference on special needs education: access and quality*. UNESCO and the Ministry of Education, Spain. Paris: UNESCO. UNESCO (1999a) *From special needs education to education for all*. A Discussion Document. Tenth Steering Committee Meeting, UNESCO, Paris, September 30–October 1, 1998. Unpublished manuscript.
37 Ainscow, M. (2016) *Struggles for equity in education: the selected works of Mel Ainscow*. Abingdon: Routledge.
38 *The Salamanca statement and framework for action on special needs education*, paragraph 3, page 6. www.unesco.org/education/pdf/SALAMA_E.PDF (Retrieved August 2nd 2017 13.26 AEST).
39 UNESCO (1994) *Final report: world conference on special needs education: access and quality*. Paris: UNESCO, pages viii & ix www.unesco.org/education/pdf/SALAMA_E.PDF (Retrieved August 2nd 2017 13.26 AEST).
40 www.ohchr.org/Documents/ProfessionalInterest/crc.pdf (Retrieved August 2nd 2017 22:39 AEST).
41 See www.un.org/development/desa/disabilities/convention-on-the-rights-of-persons-with-disabilities.html (Retrieved August 1st 2017 16:49 AEST).
42 A/HRC/25/29, para. 4 and UNICEF, *The right of children with disabilities to education: a right-based approach to inclusive education* (Geneva, 2012).
43 www.ideapartnership.org/topics-database/idea-2004/267-overview-resources.html (Retrieved August 2nd 2017 23:11 AEST).
44 http://auspeld.org.au/wp-content/uploads/2012/08/Report_on_the_Review_of_DSE.pdf (Retrieved August 2nd 2017 23:22 AEST).
45 See Bauman, Z. (2004) *Wasted lives: modernity and its outcasts*. Oxford: Polity; Slee, R. (1993) The politics of integration – new sites for old practices? *Disability, Handicap & Society*, 8(4): 351–360.
46 Danforth, S. (2009) *The incomplete child: an intellectual history of learning disabilities*. New York: Peter Lang, page 1.
47 Burt, C. (1937) *The backward child*. London: University of London Press.
48 Ball, S. J. (2013) *Foucault, power and education*. Abingdon: Routledge, pages 73 & 74.

49 Tomlinson, S. (1982) *A sociology of special education*. London: Routledge and Kegan Paul.

50 See Tomlinson, S. (1985) The expansion of special education. *Oxford Review of Education*, 11(2): 157–165; Barton, L. (Ed.) (1987) *The politics of special educational needs*. Lewes: Falmer Press.

51 Kauffman, J. M. and Hallahan, D. P. (1995) *The illusion of full inclusion: a comprehensive critique of a current special education bandwagon*. Austin, TX: Pro-Ed; Kauffman, J. M. and Sasso, G. M. (2006a) Certainty, doubt, and the reduction of uncertainty. *Exceptionality*, 14(2): 109–120; Kauffman, J. M. and Sasso, G. M. (2006b) Toward ending cultural and cognitive relativism in special education. *Exceptionality*, 14(2): 65–90.

52 Farrell, M. (2006) *Celebrating the special school*. London: David Fulton.

53 Warnock, M. (1978) *Special educational needs (The Warnock Report)*. London: HMSO; Warnock, M. (2005) *Special educational needs: a new look*. London: Philosophical Society of Great Britain. Impact Number 11, pages 43 & 48.

54 Ainscow, M. (2007) Towards a more inclusive education system. Where next for special schools? In R. Cigman (Ed.) *Included or excluded? The challenge of the mainstream for some SEN children*. London: Routledge, pages 128–139, page 128.

55 Fleck, L. (1979) *Genesis and development of a scientific fact*. Chicago: University of Chicago Press.

56 Tobin, R. M. and House, A. E. (2016) *DSM-5 diagnosis in the schools*. New York: Guildford Press.

57 Slee, R. (1993) The politics of integration – new sites for old practices? *Disability, Handicap & Society*, 8(4): 351–360. Walton, E. L. (2016) *The language of inclusive education: exploring speaking, listening, reading, and writing*. Abingdon: Routledge.

58 Bernstein, B. (1996) *Pedagogy, symbolic control and identity: theory, research, critique*. London: Taylor & Francis.

59 Rose, M. (1995) *Possible lives: the promise of public education in America*. Boston, Houghton Mifflin Co.

60 Knight, T. (1985) An apprenticeship in democracy. *The Australian Teacher*, 11(1): 5–7.

61 Henderson, B. (2011) *The blind advantage: how going blind made me a stronger principal and how including children with disabilities made our school better for everyone*. Cambridge, MA: Harvard Educational Press.

62 Hehir, T. and Katzman, L. I. (2012) *Effective inclusive schools: designing successful school-wide programs*. San Francisco: Jossey-Bass; Hehir, T. and Schifter, L. A. (2015) *How did you get here? Students with disabilities and their journeys to Harvard*. Cambridge, MA: Harvard University Press.

Interlude

Unbelievable!

In 1996 the Annual Meeting of the American Educational Research Association was held in Chicago. My wife and son travelled across from London with me. We stayed in one of the large conference hotels. These hotels are impressive and expensive. Each day we would cross the street to a diner for breakfast. This was no hardship, as we savoured the traditional American breakfast with the endless permutations for serving coffee and an egg. On one of these mornings the three of us sat in our booth, Rowan devouring what he calls *Roseanne bacon*. Across from us was a gentleman sitting alone with his copy of the *Chicago Tribune* and a "bottomless cup of coffee". Time passed.

Another man came in from the grey morning with its penetrating winds and joined the first gentleman at his table. Unravelling his scarf and draping his overcoat over the back of an empty chair, he apologised profusely for what must have been his lateness. Unconsciously, I drifted into concentration upon their ensuing conversation.

"Sorry, I was up all night watching the Oscars", said the slightly out-of-breath flush-faced man.

"No problem. I shut it down early. They always go so late and the interesting stuff is last", retorted his friend.

"Yeah, man – I should've done that too. I'm going to pay for it all day."

"So, who won the big Oscars?" enquired the first guy, beckoning the waitress to refill his cup and take their elaborate breakfast orders.

Orders taken, the waitress in an apron, who looked like someone from the film sets of my childhood, shuffled off yelling the orders to the short-order cook with his back to the patrons. She handed her boss, who sat by the register, a copy of the order from her notepad and set about resetting tables.

"*The English Patient*; best freaking film. I fell asleep in that movie!"

"Yeah, I wouldn't have picked it. *Jerry Maguire* was better, even though I can take or leave Cruise. Mostly leave", laughed the first guy surveying the very large plate set down before him.

"Unbelievable, man – Geoffrey Rush got best actor. Can you believe it? That's unbelievable".

In the nanoseconds between this last statement and the next, I noticed that I wasn't the only eavesdropper. Jeanette and Rowan were also leaning towards the table where the movie critic was holding forth. The three of us had recently seen *Shine* in a cinema just off Leicester Square and we had been moved by it.

I found myself taken up by the challenge. What's so unbelievable? Was it that David Helfgott could have a disability and be such a gifted musician? Was it the difficult relationship between the father and the son? Was it . . .

My speculations were interrupted.

"Who ever heard of an Australian concert pianist!" he explained.

Open-mouthed, three astonished Australians stared across the booth at each other.

Perspective is a funny thing.

2 Perspective, illusions and other treacheries

Finding perspective? The treachery of the image

Perhaps it's a midlife or twilight grasp at, or gasp of, creativity. Tentatively, you enrol in a drawing, a painting or an art theory class at the local community college, community centre or institution for 'hire-learning'. Inevitably you encounter the laws of perspective. Some instructors carry you back to Chinese or Greek antiquity; others will commence mid-way through early fifteenth-century Renaissance Italy with Filippo Brunelleschi to introduce the *vanishing point, one, two, three and four-point perspective*. It seems so obvious, doesn't it: objects, and the spaces between them, shrink as they recede into the distance.

The laws found expression through increasingly sophisticated geometric modelling. Robert Hughes describes the grip of perspective in *The Shock of the New*. He says:

> *"To fifteenth century artists, perspective was the philosopher's stone of art; one can hardly exaggerate the excitement they felt in the face of its ability to conjure up a measurable, precise illusion of the world".*[1]

Artists, over time, have done what artists must do – they have challenged the laws of perspective and unstitched geometric straitjackets to take command of their canvas. Others have held firm and it is very likely that your tutor will instruct you to create your parallel lines showing foreground and horizon to find the vanishing point (VP) on your canvas or sketchbook page. After all, you should learn the rules before you break them.

In superficial terms, for my understanding of art theory is entirely superficial, you will observe that the representation of the road is broad at the bottom (or *ground-line*) of the sketch and it progressively narrows as it recedes into distance. The lampposts are drawn closer together as you move into that distance and they shrink, become less clear or detailed and fainter. Where the lines of the road meet, you have found the vanishing point, and this intersects with the horizon line across the canvas.

Figure 2.1 Filippo Brunelleschi

The eye has indeed been deceived, as Robert Hughes would have it.

A quick exercise for you to test the illusion might help to demonstrate it. Take a clean sheet of paper. Draw your line representing the foreground towards the bottom of the sheet of paper. Then move your pencil towards the top of the sheet of paper and draw your horizon line. This line is parallel to the line at the bottom of the page that will represent the foreground. Between the foreground and the horizon, draw a vanishing highway. Start with the lines representing the road far apart from each other and then bring them closer together until they meet on the horizon line. You may care to draw trees or telegraph poles that are large, dark and detailed at the start of the road and become smaller and more faint as you move to the horizon. Now stare at your picture for about 60 seconds, or until you accept the appearance of distance on the sheet of plain paper. Then reach into your picture towards the horizon with your right hand. What happened? Did

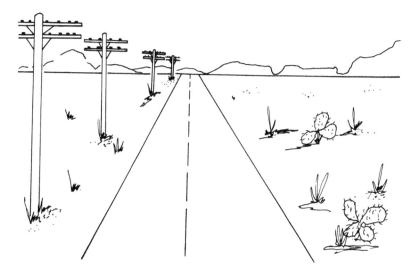

Figure 2.2 Achieving perspective

your hand, and then your arm, disappear towards the end of the road? Did you lose balance and topple down towards the end of the road? No, your hand is splayed across a still-flat piece of paper. You have broken the artist's spell.

For the sake of metaphor, I will momentarily accept the *illusion* – abide by the law of perspective in order to observe its inversion. The organisation of the education canvas, where a line has been drawn between the so-called *regular school* and the *special school* forges its own rules of perspective; its own illusions have trained our eyes to see the world in a particular manner.

According to Deborah Youdell:

> . . . it is arguable that while Special Educational Needs are often located on the fringes of education, it is in this location at the boundary that Special Educational Needs acts to define and ensure the continuity of education's normative centre.[2]

In *Foucault, power and education*, Stephen Ball elaborates the point poignantly:

> The school became in many respects an expression of humanity and a demarcation of the limits of humanity – who was and was not educable, of value, worth investing in.[3]

And so, it was that special education was the representation of a descending human value. In Bauman's terms, here is the boundary beyond which lies the surplus population. Special education, serving the so-called special educational needs of subnormal, defective and handicapped children established ableism in bricks and mortar, and ableism has endured through the organisation and institutional discourse of education. To draw from an antiquated language, the world was made up of people who were considered *valid*. And the others, you ask? Well, they were the *invalids*.

Let me pursue this for a moment more. There is nothing radical about suggesting that regular neighbourhood schools and their so-called normal children represent the foreground of the education canvas. Accordingly, as we track through the regular school corridors to the *back passages*, we will find students congregating, clutching their dossiers of diagnosis, in what are euphemistically called inclusion rooms with their special needs or inclusion teacher or more typically an assistant. Track even further back towards the vanishing point of the education canvas – *the special school* – and you will find that the detail applied to illustrate or describe these children enlarges them through elaborate detail according to the reductive representation of humanity to be found in the pages of the *Diagnostic and Statistical Manual of Mental Disorders (DSM – 5)*.[4] The representation of the so-called special needs children or students with disabilities marks them out in greater distinctiveness – in bolder, difficult-to-erase lines, but the representations are radically incomplete and hollowing, a caricature of their humanity. Nevertheless, this purely technical rendition of the child is pervasive and powerful; it has antiquity and ubiquity on its side.[5]

Notwithstanding the transgression to optic logic by this enlargement of detail and the heaviness of the lines as we move to the nether regions of the education canvas, we have accepted the illusion; this is reality.

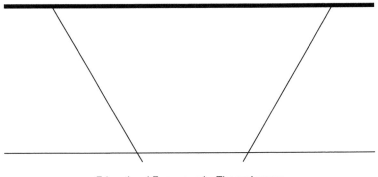

Educational Foreground – The maingame

Figure 2.3 Representation of education perspective

Counter-intuitively, the objects are enlarged with distance. And, as we have observed in our depiction of the metaphor, illusion is the point of art. So, we forgive this error and collude with its propagators.

Educational vanishing points – horizons of hopelessness

Think about Laurence Stephen Lowry's inhabitants of industrial Manchester, Bury, Salford, Rochdale and Burnley in England's northern county of Lancashire.[6] The brush line figures that populate his paintings are simultaneously crude and magnificent representations of humanity. Though they lack detail and precise form, we forgive and we celebrate Lowry for his invention. We enter a silent pact with the artist to see ourselves in his cityscapes made glorious by their austere depiction and celebration of the mundane ritual of work and leisure.

Figure 2.4 "Going to Work", L.S. Lowry, 1943

Marc Chagall's lovers are permitted to hover. Suspended between heaven and earth, we let them float.

The surrealist artist René François Ghislain Magritte is uncompromising in his reminder of *The Treachery of Images, 1929*. Underneath a bold and realistic representation of a pipe, he paints the words: "Ceci n'est pas une pipe". (Translation: This is not a pipe). He reminds us of the complicity

Figure 2.5 "Over the Town", Marc Chagall, 1918

of the artist and the viewer in accepting the arrangement of oil, colour, lines and brushstrokes as something more than it really is. This is the time-honoured power of illusion we grant the artist.

Illusion, as Pierre Bourdieu reminded us, is not the sole dominion of the artist. He asks:

> *What is meant by institutions? They are an organised fiduciary, organised trust, organised belief, **a collective fiction recognised by belief and thereby becoming real**. Clearly, to say of a reality that it is a collective fiction is a manner of saying that it has a tremendous existence, **but not as people believe it exists.**[7]*
>
> **(*My emphasis*)**

We agree on many *collective fictions* in institutional life, don't we? Some cornerstone assumptions of schooling are illustrative. Consider the following:

- The school curriculum is best constructed by dividing and organising knowledge into discrete disciplines such as history, geography, science, art, mathematics, language and so forth.

Figure 2.6 "The Treachery of Images", Rene Magritte, 1929

- Children learn best by being organised into groups, grades or classes according to their age or, as Ken Robinson says, "Their date of manufacture".
- Testing children's memory of the content of lessons is a measure of their ability and vocational aptitude.
- The Bell Curve has scientific legitimacy and is an accurate measure and predictor of individual "*intelligence*".
- Children with disabilities learn best when they are grouped together, often according to diagnostic category – much like it is in hospital, away from students who don't have disabilities.
- Children with disabilities learn better when in separate schools away from so called ordinary or *normal* children.

Building collective fictions and losing perspective?

In 1974 the British government appointed a committee of enquiry Chaired by Mary Warnock a senior research fellow from Oxford to "*review educational provision in England, Scotland and Wales for children and young people handicapped by disabilities of body or mind, taking account of the medical aspects of their needs, together with arrangements to prepare them for entry into employment: to consider the most effective use of resources for these purposes; and to make recommendations*".[8] As far as I know, the term *special educational needs* first appeared in Dame Mary Warnock's 1978 Report. From that point, it took a foothold in the educational lexicon and psyche. Its global reach and endurance is remarkable. However, its most common usage is not as the committee of enquiry had intended. In their critical review of the impacts of the *Warnock Report* Len Barton and Maeve Landman confirm the report's challenge to *"medical notions of handicap"* and its introduction of a concept of a *"continuum of educational needs. It confirmed the perspective that the purpose and goals of education for all children are the same"*.[9] *Special Educational Needs* is simultaneously an object of and vehicle for profound reductionism. In its most common and enduring usage, *special educational needs* became a shorthand reference for the cohort of defective children in school systems around the world. It is also a pejorative reference in effect – essentially ableist. Of course, many able-bodied people will reject the negative overtones of the term of reference. They have never been referred to or had their lives organised into special education needs.

Four decades after its application by the British committee of enquiry, educators and the community alike use *special educational needs* to describe ever-expanding groups of people, places and programmes. Put simply, *special educational needs* has become a part of the institutional fabric of twentieth and twenty-first-century education. Teachers, education administrators and support workers, parents, students and the media all apply this term of reference to an increasing range of children experiencing difficulties at school. Not surprisingly, the term is taken to have a common meaning on face value, but it is used variously. *Special educational needs*, or its derivatives – *special needs children* and *SEN*, describes the clientele (Special Needs or SEN students), the practitioners (Special Needs Teachers, Special Needs Assistants, Special Needs Coordinators), the training programmes (Masters of Special Educational Needs, Graduate Diploma of Special Educational Needs), the educational sites (the special needs room, the special needs school, the special educational needs annex), the administrative section (the Office of Special Educational Needs) and of course, the section in the special needs shelves in the library and the book shops.

In simple terms, we could represent *special educational needs* like a software programme icon that, when opened, reveals an elaborate web of diagnostic categories that describe the so-called special educational needs, or more colloquially – the special needs, child. It is a detailed matrix with finer grains of distinction to assist in making decisions about children's education and their ensuing options, or restricted choices, for life. It is important to note that this not static. Glacier metaphors seem appropriate as it inches its way forward over time. Figure 2.7 indicates the first "drop down" of categories within the Special Educational Needs classification.

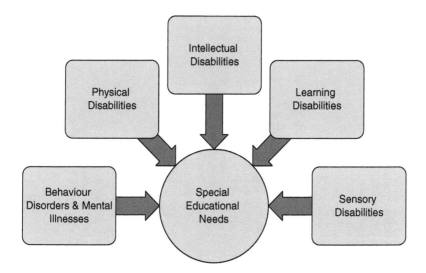

Figure 2.7 Special educational needs diagnostic categories

Each diagnostic classification: Behaviour Disorders & Mental Illnesses, Physical Disabilities, Cognitive Disabilities, Specific Learning Disorders, and Sensory Disabilities, has its own set of diagnostic sub-categories. Figure 2.8 offers an indicative snapshot of the next tier of calibrations that contains a selection of sub-categories just from the behaviour disorders and mental illnesses and learning disabilities classifications. A similar diagram could be drawn for each of these general classifications, each with its cascading calibrations therein. I instance behaviour disorders and mental illnesses and learning disabilities as they represent the fastest growing areas of special educational needs diagnoses.

As an aside, the gifted and talented child is also frequently described as a "special educational needs child". It could be said that SEN is reaching into both ends of the Bell Curve (Figure 2.9) and eyeing off the middle ground all the while. We have witnessed the movement of SEN classifications and diagnoses into the bulk of the population that is represented as the bulky middle of the Bell Curve.[10]

As a diagrammatic representation of population ability distribution, the Bell Curve has lost any lingering credibility, following the racist assertions of Herrnstein and Murray,[11] as well as its shape. The Bell Curve is rendered redundant in the contemporary educational landscape.[12] Like the Bell Curve, Special Educational Needs is as Bourdieu tells us, a collective

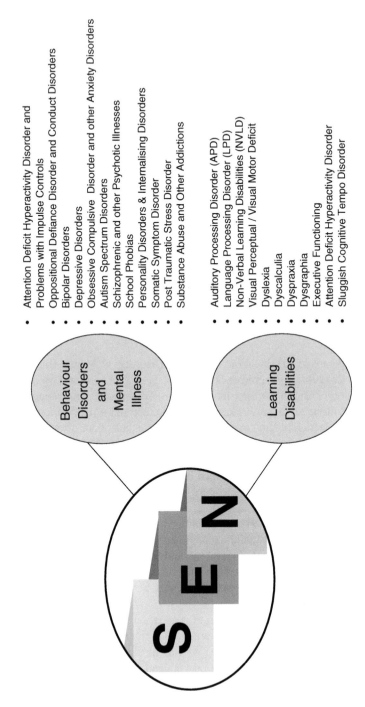

Behaviour Disorders and Mental Illness

- Attention Deficit Hyperactivity Disorder and Problems with Impulse Controls
- Oppositional Defiance Disorder and Conduct Disorders
- Bipolar Disorders
- Depressive Disorders
- Obsessive Compulsive Disorder and other Anxiety Disorders
- Autism Spectrum Disorders
- Schizophrenic and other Psychotic Illnesses
- School Phobias
- Personality Disorders & Internalising Disorders
- Somatic Symptom Disorder
- Post Traumatic Stress Disorder
- Substance Abuse and Other Addictions

Learning Disabilities

- Auditory Processing Disorder (APD)
- Language Processing Disorder (LPD)
- Non-Verbal Learning Disabilities (NVLD)
- Visual Perceptual / Visual Motor Deficit
- Dyslexia
- Dyscalculia
- Dyspraxia
- Dysgraphia
- Executive Functioning
- Attention Deficit Hyperactivity Disorder
- Sluggish Cognitive Tempo Disorder

Figure 2.8 SEN behaviour disorders & mental illness and learning disabilities

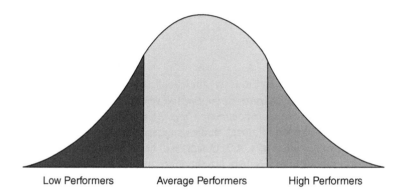

Low Performers   Average Performers   High Performers

Figure 2.9 The bell curve

fiction – an organised trust or belief made strong through years of utterance, usage and ill-considered acceptance.[13]

Sally Tomlinson first expressed her concern about both the exponential expansion of the statutory categories of disability used by education authorities in England and Wales and the disproportionate referral of Black British students to special educational services in Educational *Subnormality: A study in decision making* with elaboration in *A Sociology of Special Education* in 1982.[14] Although called to account by numerous researchers in North America and England,[15] special education has failed to adequately address the fact of racial overrepresentation. Tomlinson's concern has certainly not diminished since her work in the last century. In fact, she is more concerned about the correspondence of the inexorable *manufacture of inability* through the machinations of increasingly competitive schools, the evaporation of the unskilled labour market and the growth of the special educational needs industry. There's an old joke that tickled me as a schoolboy. *How do you know if there's an elephant in the shower with you? You can smell the peanuts on his breath.* The racialization of special needs is certainly an elephant in the classroom and we have failed to acknowledge and take responsibility for the cloying smell of peanuts.

Warnock first offered the term *special educational needs* to dislodge the hold of the medical model of disability across the educational establishment. Special educational needs was appropriated and applied by the special education fraternity to deflect from business as usual. '*Special educational needs*' is now offered unflinchingly as a part of the lexicon of inclusive education. Let us conclude our discussion of the establishment of illusion in the language and practice of education by recognition of and reference to the growing pressure to further calibrate the student population according to their bio-identities.

'*Psychiatry Online*'

Renee Tobin and Alvin House's guidebook, *DSM-5 Diagnosis in the Schools*, promises to "*increase school-based practitioners' familiarity with DSM-5 and to bolster their confidence in using it within school settings*".[16] They report on epidemiological studies suggesting that between 180 and 220 students in a cohort of 1,000 students will have diagnosable psychiatric disorders. School psychologists are therefore expected to play a frontline role in the psychiatric diagnosis of students. They are gatekeeping for reimbursement decisions made by insurance companies and government agencies.[17] *DSM-5*, when correctly followed and applied, provides the blueprint for these diagnostic decisions. Not only does the *DSM-5* provide a diagnostic classification, it provides a corresponding numerical code (ICD-9-CM) for insurance reimbursement decisions in the USA.[18]

© Michael Leunig

For those who are unaware of *DSM (The Diagnostic and Statistical Manual of Mental Disorders)* in its various incarnations, it is a diagnostic manual compiled by successive Task Forces of the American Psychiatric Association (APA). The first edition of *DSM* was published in 1952 under the guidance of George Raines, a former navy neuropsychiatrist and professor of psychiatry at Georgetown University. Known as DSM-I, it was subject to a series of revisions. *DSM-II* was published in 1968, followed by *DSM-III* in 1980 marking a move from psychotherapy to psychobiology.[19] Seven years later an edited update, *DSM-III-R*, was published with little substantive revision. *DSM-IV* followed in 1994 with little substantive change and was succeeded by further text revisions, *DSM-IV*-TR in 2000. *DSM-5* was published in 2013. It seems significant that Professor Allen Frances who was the Chairman of the *DSM-IV* Task Force has been a vociferous critic of *DSM-5*. His criticisms encompass procedural and methodological issues, conceptual tensions, fiduciary conflicts and its actual and potential deleterious impacts.

Visit the website, https://psychiatryonline.org and you encounter the American Psychiatric Association's (APA) catalogue of publications which is headlined by *DSM-5* and its associated products. For Frances, herein lies the conflict of interest:

> *"All along, APA has treated DSM-5 more as private publishing asset than as public trust. First there were confidentiality agreements to protect "intellectual property", then an inappropriately aggressive protection of trademark and copyright, and finally the unseemly rush to prematurely publish because this was necessary to fill a budgetary hole. APA has an impossible conflict of interest in its dual role as fiduciary of the diagnostic system (a public trust) and beneficiary of publishing profits. Guild interest should never trump public interest – but it has.*[20]

DSM-5 is a complicated manual comprising three sections: DSM-5 Basics, Diagnostic Criteria and Codes, and Emerging Measures and Models. In Section II there are 20 groups of disorders and a discussion of *"other conditions and problems that may be a focus of clinical attention or that may otherwise affect the diagnosis, course, prognosis, or treatment of a patient's mental disorder"*.[21] The groups of disorders are listed in Table 2.1

DSM-5 is, according to Frances, hostage to faddism:

> *"DSM-5 has included several sure-fire fads of the future. All have symptoms that are part of everyday life and commonly encountered in the general population. None has a definition precise enough to prevent the*

Table 2.1 DSM-5 Classifications

Neurodevelopmental Disorders	Schizophrenia Spectrum and Other Psychotic Disorders	Bipolar and Related Disorders	Anxiety Disorders	Obsessive-Compulsive and Related Disorders	Trauma- and Stressor-Related Disorders	Dissociative Disorders
Somatic Symptom and Related Disorders	Feeding and Eating Disorders	Elimination Disorders	Sleep-Wake Disorders	Sexual Dysfunctions	Gender Dysphoria	Disruptive, Impulse-Control, and Conduct Disorders
Substance-Relative and Addictive Disorders	Neurocognitive Disorders	Personality Disorders	Paraphilic Disorders	Other Mental Disorders	Medication-Induced Movement Disorders and Other Adverse Effects of Medication	*Other conditions and problems that may be a focus of clinical attention or that may otherwise affect the diagnosis, course, prognosis, or treatment of a patient's mental disorder*

mislabelling of many people now considered normal. None has a treatment proven to be effective. All will likely lead to much unnecessary, and sometimes harmful, treatment or testing. The aggregate effects will be over diagnosis, unnecessary stigma, overtreatment, a misallocation of resources, and a negative impact in the way we see ourselves as individuals and as a society".[22]

He instances Disruptive Mood Dysregulation Disorder (DMDD), earlier referred to as "temper disregulation", to illustrate his point about unnecessary diagnosis.

"The idea of turning temper tantrums into a mental disorder is terrible, however named. We should not have the ambition to label as mental disorder every inconvenient or distressing aspect of childhood".[23]

© Michael Leunig

This essay did not set out to deliver clear judgements about *DSM*. Paradoxically, the *DSM* project reinforces the fact that difference is the *normal* condition of humankind. Attempts to classify and regulate standards of behaviour reach into realms of normative conjecture: musings about the nature and manifestations of normality and the activity of everyday life. Making sense of symptoms, determining attribution and recommending specific treatments, as diagnosticians from Abraham Flexner onwards have told us, is no simple matter. Attempts to make it simple often end in tears as we endure the consequences of our reductionist urges. The evolution of *DSM* is a reflection of the changing world of which it is a part.

Its ubiquity through its multiple platforms – hard copies including translations from English into 21 other languages, e-book, APPs, website – has made it accessible and its use difficult to manage. It resides in a world where our somatic and bio-identities have become a major preoccupation in the quest to optimise health and vitality, and to support each other through impairment, illness or disorder-based self-help groups.[24] Such organisations exhibit all of the attributes and actions of thought collectives, described by Ludwik Fleck,[25] as they agitate for recognition, research and revenue. Disorders are no longer discussed in seclusion and whispers. Talk-back radio, blogs, glossy magazines, docudramas, soap operas, reality, current affairs and human-interest television, school and kindergarten drop-off and pick-up points, work staffrooms and canteens, classrooms, church meetings, sporting clubs, conferences, and training workshops are just some of the platforms for the mass communication, and miscommunication, of information about mental illness and disorders. Supporting this interest is the rise of what is commonly referred to as *brain science*.[26] We could reasonably say that there is a hyper awareness of, and new receptiveness to, mental illness and disorders. It is within this milieu that *DSM* finds a mutuality of interest.

Discussions like this are riddled with paradox. As Dan Goodley observes, education polices citizenship and identity.[27] The notion of normality is fluid. People turn to diagnoses of their children to secure resources that will support their education. Ironically you have the move into what would be described as categories of disability as well as a reach for a diagnosis of "gifted and talented". Normality has outlived its utility. Lennard Davis considers "the demise of the concept of normality" this way:

> *Is it possible that normal, in its largest sense, which has done such heavy lifting in the area of eugenics, scientific racism, ableism, gender bias, homophobia, and so on, is playing itself out and losing its utility as a driving force in culture in general and academic culture in particular? And if normal is being decommissioned as a discursive organiser, what replaces it? I will argue that in its place the term diverse serves as the new normalising term. Another way of putting this point, somewhat tautologically, is that diversity is the new normality.*[28]

Rather than attempt to rule a line under our discussion of *DSM*, I will leave it in an unsatisfactory state of suspension with some tentative suggestions. First, there exists great controversy around *DSM* in its various iterations and effects. While I have drawn from Frances, he is not alone. Robert Whitaker registered early warnings concerning the conflicted pecuniary reliance on the pharmaceutical industry.[29] His early misgivings about the role of the APA in the "astonishing rise" of mental illness in America have escalated over time.[30] Kutchins and Kirk assert that while "the constant revising provides the illusion that knowledge is changing rapidly and that more specific categories are likely to be more valid and used more reliably", a more accurate assessment is gained from analysis of the power struggles within the APA and psychiatry at large.[31] The revisions they say chart the attempts of psychiatry to reach into everyday life and claim it as illness. In his circumnavigation of the "American Psyche's" global travels, Ethan Watters demonstrates the cultural foundations of *DSM* and its struggle against local interpretations of normality and disorder.[32] Joel Paris and James Philips host an interesting examination of the *DSM-5* and psychiatric nosology. One of their contributors, Edward Shorter, reinforces Watters dictum; "*The DSM series is more a cultural than a scientific document*".[33]

Second, the borders between a mild disorder and the absence of that disorder are fuzzy and highly interpretable. Accordingly, causation is not an exact science for precise calculation. The procedural guidance for the application of diagnoses suggests otherwise. *DSM* has its illusory life. The user accepts the assumptions of the manual and the rules for its application and thenceforth too its conclusions about mind and behaviour. Indeed, there has been a move to create *shadow syndromes* to enable diagnosis and treatment when the symptoms do not quite meet the requirements for a *DSM* diagnosis. Questions shuffle forward. How far are we prepared to look outside of the pathology of the child and the contents of *DSM* to form explanations for interactions between children and their complex contexts that they move in and out of?

Third, should *DSM*, or its creators and custodians, take some level of responsibility for being an antidote for educational failure (sic. the failure of education). The National Rifle Association of America's defence – "It's not the gun, it's the lunatic that's using it" – is not acceptable. Not acceptable for the timidity of the American Senate and Congress expressed by its failure to introduce restrictions to gun ownership or a failure to reform the highly competitive neo-liberal culture of schooling and its inexorable press for the relentless calibration of school populations. *Special needs* or a seemingly more sensitive rendition: *additional needs* are bureaucratic illusions. At what point does need become additional and or special? They are certainly not stable constructs. They are management techniques and though the packaging becomes ever-more sophisticated, the assumptions remain crude.

Fourth, and not surprisingly, mental illness manifestation and causation is uniquely individual. Joel Paris describes it this way:

> *The Robins/Guze notion of two individuals having the same disorder because they share the same disorder phenotype will, technically, not be realised. Oddly, in a very strict sense every individual with psychiatric illness will have his or her own unique causal picture and his own disorder.*[34]

DSM attempts to standardise *post hoc* – it forms a shaky science that becomes the basis for the classification and management of students who trouble, or are troubled by, the cultures, structures and operation of a school system long past its use by date.

Before we return to the artist's studio, let us briefly consider findings from Australia's Commonwealth Department of Health. The Report of the Second Australian Child and Adolescent Survey of Mental Health and Wellbeing, *The Mental Health of Children and Adolescents*, was published in August 2015. It reported on a national survey wherein 76,606 households were approached and visited up to six times between June 2013 and April 2014.[35] The findings from the survey are simultaneously alarming, instructive and perplexing. Questions arise, not just about the psychopathology of children and adolescents themselves, although this is certainly warranted, but also about the overlapping contingencies that affect the mental health of children and adolescents. Might I say, without denying biology, that mental health is contingent?

Almost 1 in 7 (13.9%) of 4- to 17-year-olds were assessed as having mental disorders in the previous 12 months – equivalent to 560,000 Australian children and adolescents. ADHD was the most common mental disorder in children and adolescents – 298,000 in the previous 12 months (7.4%). Two-thirds of these children and adolescents with ADHD (65.7%) had mild forms of the disorder. As we have said, it is at the margins of having and not having a mental disorder that the cracks in the scientific edifice emerge.

This is not to deny difference and disorder, I am instantiating it. Difference is now and has always been the human condition. Institutions forge standardised structures and practices. Difference is a disruptor to be managed. Exclusion has hitherto been applied through relatively blunt instruments. As is the case in all spheres of this twenty-first-century existence, sophistication is a hallmark. My family and friends laugh at me for buying music on compact discs (they have stopped laughing at my enduring penchant for vinyl). Special education is resilient and predatory. It is ahead of the game in staking its claim in both the segregated network of "special" (now specialist) schools and the neighbourhood school. The confluence of a range of social, political and economic factors in the age of virtual knowledge making, DSM and the brain sciences has pressed special education to refine its branding and practices. It has not fundamentally reformed its assumptions about standard and abnormal childhood and adolescent development. The language of special and additional needs, like the laws of perspective in art, form an illusion. Sadly, inclusive education by failing to establish and protect strong conceptual boundaries is all too often an illusion. Exclusion by any name remains exclusion.

Notes

1 Hughes, R. (1991) *The shock of the new: art and the century of change*. London: Thames & Hudson, page 16.
2 Youdell, D. (2006) *Impossible bodies, impossible selves exclusions and student subjectivities*. Dordrecht: Springer, page 22.
3 Ball, S. J. (2013) *Foucault, power, and education*. New York: Routledge, page 48.
4 American Psychiatric Association (2013) *Diagnostic and statistical manual of mental disorders: DSM-5*. Arlington, VA: American Psychiatric Association.
5 Slee, R. (2011) *The irregular school*. Abingdon: Routledge.
6 Berger, J. (1966) Lowry and the industrial north. In J. Berger (1980) *About looking*. London: Bloomsbury, pages 94–102.
7 Bourdieu, P. (2014) *On the state: lectures at the Collège de France, 1989–1992*. Cambridge: Polity, page 37.
8 Department of Education and Science (1978) *Special educational needs: report of the committee of enquiry into the education of handicapped children and young people (Warnock Report)*. London: Her Majesty's Stationery Office, page 1.
9 Barton, L. and Landman, M. (1993) The politics of integration: Observations on the Warnock Report. In R. Slee (Ed.) *Is there a desk with my name on it?* Lewes: Falmer Press.
10 Tomlinson, S. (2017) *A sociology of special and inclusive education: exploring the manufacture of inability*. Abingdon: Routledge. Tomlinson, S. (2013) *Ignorant yobs? Low attainers in a global knowledge economy*. New York: Routledge.
11 Herrnstein, R. J. and Murray, C. A. (1994) *The bell curve: intelligence and class structure in American life*. London: Simon & Schuster, 1996.
12 Black-Hawkins, K., Florian, L. and Rouse, M. (2017) *Achievement and inclusion in schools*. London: Routledge.
13 Op. cit. (Bourdieu, 2014), page 37.
14 Tomlinson, S. (1981) *Educational subnormality: a study in decision-making*. London: Routledge & Kegan Paul; Tomlinson, S. (1982) *A sociology of special education*. London: Routledge and Kegan Paul.
15 Parrish, T. (2005) Racial disparities in the identification, funding and provision of special education. In D. J. Losen and G. Orfield. (Eds.) *Racial inequality in special education*. Cambridge: Harvard Education Press, pages 15–37; Harry, B. (2014) The disproportionate placement of ethnic minorities in special education. In L. Florian (Ed.) *The Sage handbook of special education*. London: Sage, Volume 1, pages 73–95; Gillborn, D. (2008) *Racism and education: coincidence*

or conspiracy? London: Routledge; Dyson, A. and Kozleski, E. B. (2008) Disproportionality in special education – a transatlantic phenomenon. In L. Florian and M. J. McLaughlin (Eds.) *Disability classifications in education: issues and perspectives*. Thousand Oaks, CA: Corwin Press, pages 170–190; Tomlinson, S. (2017) *A sociology of special and inclusive education: exploring the manufacture of inability*. Abingdon: Routledge.

16 Tobin, R. M. and House, A. E. (2016) *DSM-5 diagnosis in the schools*. New York: Guildford Press, page 1.

17 Ibid., page 10.

18 Ibid., page 10.

19 Paris, J. and Phillips, J. (Eds.) (2013) *Making the DSM-5*. Dordrecht: Springer, page 9.

20 Frances, A. (2013) *Saving normal: an insider's revolt against out-of-control psychiatric diagnosis, DSM-5, big pharma, and the medicalization of ordinary life*. New York: William Morrow, page 176.

21 American Psychiatric Association (2013) *Diagnostic and statistical manual of mental disorders: DSM-5*. Arlington, VA: American Psychiatric Association, page 715.

22 Frances, A. (2013) *Saving normal: an insider's revolt against out-of-control psychiatric diagnosis, DSM-5, big pharma, and the medicalization of ordinary life*. New York: William Morrow, page 176.

23 Ibid., page 177.

24 Rose, N. (2007) *Politics of life itself: biomedicine, power and subjectivity in the twenty-first century*. Princeton, NJ: Princeton University Press.

25 Fleck, L. (1979) *Genesis and development of a scientific fact*. Chicago: University of Chicago Press.

26 The implied singularity of the term *brain science* is misleading, as what is more precisely referred to as brain sciences is a very broad church wherein many disciplines and interests gather. These gatherings reflect strong coalitions of interest and belief as well as deep divisions. I will simply refer you to the work of the eminent biologist Steven Rose for insight into the nature of these epistemological ruptures. See Rose, S. P. R. (2005) *The 21st-century brain: explaining, mending and manipulating the mind*. London: Jonathan Cape. Also Rose, H. and Rose, S. P. R. (2013) *Genes, cells and brains: the Promethean promises of the new biology*. London: Verso; and Rose, N. and Abi-Rached, J. M. (2014) Governing through the brain: neuropolitics, neuroscience and subjectivity. *Cambridge Anthropology*, 32(1): 2–23; Rose, N. and Abi-Rached, J. M. (2013) *Neuro: the new brain science and the management of the mind*. Princeton, NJ: Princeton University Press.

27 Goodley, D. (2017) *Disability studies: an interdisciplinary introduction*. London: Sage, pages 176–178. See also Ball, S. J. (2013) *Foucault, power, and education*. Abingdon: Routledge.

28 Davis, L. J. (2013) *The end of normal: identity in a biocultural era*. Ann Arbor, MI: University of Michigan Press, page 1. (Author's emphases)

29 Whitaker, R. (2002) *Mad in America: bad science, bad medicine, and the enduring mistreatment of the mentally ill*. Cambridge, MA: Perseus Publications.

30 Whitaker, R. (2010) *Anatomy of an epidemic: magic bullets, psychiatric drugs, and the astonishing rise of mental illness in America*. New York: Crown Publishers.

31 Kutchins, H. and Kirk, S. A. (1997) *Making US crazy. DSM: the psychiatric bible and the creation of mental disorders*. New York: Free Press.
32 Watters, E. (2010) *Crazy like us: the globalization of the American psyche*. New York: Free Press.
33 Shorter, E. (2013) The history of DSM. In J. Paris and J. Phillips (Eds.) *Making the DSM-5*. Dordrecht: Springer, page 17.
34 Paris, J. and Phillips, J. (Eds.) (2013) *Making the DSM-5*. Dordrecht: Springer, page 155.
35 Lawrence, D., Johnson, S., Hafekost, J., Boterhoven de Haan, K., Sawyer, M., Ainley, J. and Zubrick, S. R. (2015) *The mental health of children and adolescents: report of the second Australian child and adolescent survey of mental health and wellbeing*. Canberra: Department of Health.

Interlude

It's a long way down

"Every summer fifty thousand swimmers and layabouts click through its turnstiles. Bill Decis (the pool manager) knows, as do the parents of the area, that the neighbourhood pool is the biggest and cheapest child-minding centre ever invented".[1]

Parents in rural towns across Australia know this too. My school holidays were the days of the shimmering heat and water of the Hamilton public swimming pool. These were days spent in cool heavily chlorinated water punctuated with lying on hot concrete to warm up before illicit games of 'chasey' in the furthest perimeter of the pool grounds where the teenage lovers gathered away from the gaze and patrols of the pool manager. Every morning my mother would give my sister and me a shilling each before she set off for work. Her instructions were always the same: "Be careful, be home before dinnertime, and Roger – wear your T-shirt all day, even when you're swimming". That last command was an acknowledgement of the defencelessness of my inherited pasty English freckled skin. The shilling was split between a modest entry fee, the can of Fanta and the bag of Twisties or crisps for lunch. Twenty-first-century parents must be frowning with horror and levelling assertions of *abuse* at my careless parents. But this was the way it was for working-class kids in the 1960s who didn't go on holidays in the summer with parents who could afford it. I am not complaining, for these really were the carefree and careless formative days of my life. William Blake would no doubt smile and celebrate its innocence.

There were occasions when I took my shirt off to reveal sunburn and blisters from a day of swimming without the protection of the shirt in the water. In mitigation, the pain of sunburn and the scalding of a frustrated mother hurt less than the taunts of my friends whose skin took on the appearance of a well-worn brown leather bag. Being different was not a good look.

The pool had a 'babies' pool' for mums to dip infants in. We would walk through it en-route to the big pool to cool our feet from the long walk across town to get to the pool. Sometimes the manager would shout at us, "Get out of there". I am reaching back through the fog of some 50-odd years, but I see a low brick and stone structure that divided the Olympic-sized swimming pool from the wading pool for very young children who couldn't swim. My sister and I usually separated once we arrived. She would go up onto the grassy bank where the older kids hung out, sunbaking, smoking and planning nocturnal liaisons. I would meet my friends and throw my clothes and towel close to the pool at the shallow end. There wasn't a written rule, but it was understood that weak and non-swimmers weren't allowed past the mid-pool ladders around the "four-foot" depth mark. Of course, this was an invitation. The gravitational pull of the "ten-foot" end dragged us along the internal guttering. We would hold on to the gutter edge and sometimes flounder in the deeper waters when the strong swimmers prised open our grip on the poolside or the ladders. Of necessity, we became swimmers quickly. I still use that inelegant version of the Australian Crawl that lacks the grace and economy of my children's swimming club–honed strokes.

Once secure in the deep end, the diving boards presented themselves as challenges. First, the 1-meter springboard beckoned, which gave way to the call of its 3-meter companion. Like my friends, I would nervously scale the ladder and spend time on the waiting end of the diving board. The view was great. When no one else was on the board, I would inch my way to the end and peer down at the water. I would then step back and climb down the ladder to enter the pool less conspicuously, less courageously. Like others, I did this frequently. There were times when someone would stand on the board and urge me to dive. I would brush past them telling them to go first. Bigger kids would stand in menacing defiance blocking the way back. At first, I would jump. Eventually I dived and I dived and I dived. There was no going back. It was life-changing. I spent summers in the queue waiting for my turn to perfect my modest pikes or the largest splash I could manage as a 4-foot, 4.5-stone Adonis.

Note

1 This is an extract from Helen Garner's Aqua Profonda. See Garner, H. (1996) *True stories*. Melbourne: Text Publishing Melbourne, pages 223–228, page 223.

3   Diving for dear life[1]

A remark you made[2]

As is her way, the One Nation Party senator Pauline Hanson outraged sections of the Australian public with comments about children with disabilities and autism in her explanatory remarks for siding with the conservative Liberal government's education funding reform bill during its reading in the Senate chamber. For the international reader, Pauline Hanson is the leader of the One Nation Party.[3] The One Nation Party contested the last federal election on a platform of restricting immigration, halting the building of new mosques across Australia and commissioning "an enquiry into Islam". The last plank in this platform of division is curious and potentially confusing. It must not be interpreted as an invitation to build greater understanding of Islam and its many followers in our community. It was an incendiary proposal designed to sweep up the disenchanted, marginalised and growing numbers of economically redundant white people who would readily target immigrants as the cause of their economic and social vulnerabilities. The senator even excited outrage from her most conservative colleagues in the Senate when she wore a burqa in the Senate chamber to incite hostility towards the Muslim community. Hanson and her One Nation Party are of course not the only ones to resort to immigration and Australian identity politics to bolster electoral favour. Most parties in Australian politics have drawn from this well, and no doubt they will continue to do so.

In Queensland's daily newspaper, *The Courier Mail*, Matthew Killoran reported that Senator Pauline Hanson, in announcing her party's support for the government's school funding package, had said that disabled and autistic children should be removed from the *normal* classroom for the benefit of the other children so that they can get the special attention they need and not monopolise the *normal* classroom teachers' time and thereby impede the progress of the other children.[4]

The outcry was quick and it came from all directions. Federal House of Representatives Labor Party member Emma Husar is the mother of Mitch,

(Photo taken from *The Sydney Morning Herald*, August 17, 2017 at www.smh.com.au/federal-politics/political-news/one-nation-leader-pauline-hanson-wears-full-burqa-in-senate-question-time-stunt-20170817-gxyd5d.html)

a 10-year-old boy with autism. She was forthright in her condemnation of Hanson's remarks and called for an apology from the senator to all people in Australia with autism. She then directed her comments to the 164,000 Australians who have an autism spectrum disorder. "Even on the days that are hard – when you're frustrated and your disability makes you angry – you are still better than she is on her best day", said Emma Husar.[5]

Husar, joined by numerous other parliamentarians, called for an apology and a retraction of the "bigoted" remarks. This is encapsulated when the following day in the Federal Senate Queensland Labor Senator, Murray Watt commenced *Questions Without Notice* with a question to the Liberal Party Minister for Education, Senator Simon Birmingham:

> *My question is to the Minister for Education and Training, Senator Birmingham. Yesterday Senator Hanson told the Senate that students living with a disability or diagnosed with autism 'are taking up the teacher's time' in the classroom and should 'go into a special classroom'. So far, the minister has been silent. Why is the minister refusing to repudiate Senator Hanson's offensive and discriminatory comments?*[6]

Senator Birmingham, deflecting points of order by Senators Penny Wong, Douglas Cameron and Katy Gallagher and defended by the President of the

Senate Stephen Parry, referred to the government's implementation of the Disability Standards in Education, a requirement of the Disability Discrimination Act (1992) and to their attention to maintaining a targeted funding scheme to ensure inclusive education in Australian schools without repudiating the remarks from Senator Hanson.[7] A government with the slimmest of majorities plays a cautious game with the minority parties and independent members on the cross benches no matter how deplorable their statements are.

Outside of the Australian parliament all major media outlets were alight with the controversy ignited by Senator Hanson's call for disabled and autistic children to be excluded from *normal* mainstream classrooms. Parents of children with a diagnosis of autism in particular and disabilities in general registered their condemnations through media outlets. A prominent and popular media identity, Waleed Aly was moved to speak of his own 9-year-old son, Zayd, who had been diagnosed with autism in 2011. Condemning Hanson's speech in the Senate, he said:

> "One of the problems with autism – and one of the problems with what Pauline Hanson said about it yesterday – it's not that it's never true that it can be really difficult for teachers. But it's that the experience of autism is so diverse that you can't possibly categorise it in this way."[8]

Stephanie Gotlib, the Chief Executive Officer of Children and Young People with Disability Australia (CYDA), published an opinion piece on the Australian Broadcasting Commission's (ABC) website entitled: *Gonski 2.0: Pauline Hanson's insensitive remarks aren't the only bad news for disabled students.*[9] Gotlib writes:

> *They (Senator Hanson's remarks) are a reminder of the entrenched culture of low expectations and the discriminatory attitudes that result in students with disability being denied access to an inclusive, quality education.*

Gotlib goes on to refute the claim that an inclusive education for students with disabilities or autism jeopardises the progress of students without disabilities or autism in the classroom:

> *Access to an inclusive education is a human right for every Australian child. There is a very clear and overwhelming evidence base that demonstrates inclusive education is enriching for students with and without disability.*

Social media including Facebook discussion groups, disability advocacy organisations, academics and interested individuals registered their opposition. Twitter was also agitated with tweets of support for and opposition to Senator Hanson. Senator Hanson rose in the Senate the next day to clarify her remarks, rather than to apologise. Her view was that her remarks were seriously misconstrued and misrepresented. So, let us return to Senator Hanson's transcript of her clarification to the parliament for the sake of accuracy. The extract is long, but it is important to cite it in full to avoid selective bias in the representation of her remarks.[10]

Senator Hanson
(Queensland) (18:36):   I am glad you have raised this, because I think you are totally misled. You are misinforming this parliament. I never said that children with autism would not be in normal, average schools. I said that they should actually have a special classroom. They should have a classroom where they actually have the special attention that they need with the teachers.

Senator Hanson-Young interjecting –

Senator Hanson: I have actually had a lot of comments from teachers who are contacting my office and are saying that it is clearly a problem in the classrooms that has not been addressed. Parents are also saying, 'It is a great idea and thank goodness someone has finally opened up the debate on this and actually wants to discuss it'. Anyway, we have had a lot of support today from people who believe this must be opened for debate. All children deserve a decent education, and I think what the government has done in this bill to increase the funding for autism in schools is a wonderful idea. I believe it has gone from approximately $690 million up to $1.23 billion, so that is much appreciated, especially by Giant Steps – they are very appreciative of it. Giant Steps is a school for autistic children. Their parents had trouble getting them into schools and they did not fit into schools, and that is why Giant Steps has been started.

There is another thing. I had a letter from a 15-year-old boy today, and he said: 'You are right in what you said. I went to a state school and I was bullied. I was not treated properly and I was left out of excursions, to the point I felt like I could die. It was not till mum found me a Catholic school for special kids that I then started to learn properly. I felt accepted and I went on excursions'.

I think what is important is this: let's have the debate about it. There clearly is a problem. Because I raised an issue, you have misled this parliament about what my true statements were. You were not interested – through the Chair. I do not believe the Greens or the Labor Party are interested in what I have to say. I think it has been political point scoring. Parents and children have heard these comments. They have been taken completely out of context.

Everyone deserves a decent education. As I said in part of my speech – *I wish I had it here to say it word for word* – if it were one of my children I would want them to have all the special needs and attention that they truly deserve. Do not throw the baby out with the bathwater. Look at the problems out there. Listen to what the people are saying. Listen to what the teachers are saying. Even the Queensland Teachers' Union admits there is a problem with autism in the classrooms – that teachers are not taught or qualified in how to handle this. That has to be addressed.[11] (My emphasis)

As is so often the case with statements of clarification, the hole is dug deeper. Let us go back to the day before and to the offending speech; "*word for word*":

Senator Hanson: *There is another thing that we need to address, and I will go back to the classrooms again. I hear so many times from parents and teachers whose time is taken up with children – whether they have a disability or whether they are autistic – who are taking up the teacher's time in the classroom. These kids have a right to an education, by all means, but, if there are a number of them, these children should go into a special classroom and be looked after and given that special attention. Because most of the time the teacher spends so much time on them they forget about the child who is straining at the bit and wants to go ahead in leaps and bounds in their education. That child is held back by those others, because the*

> teachers spend time with them. I am not denying
> them. If it were one of my children I would love all
> the time given to them to give them those opportuni-
> ties. But it is about the loss for our other kids. I think
> that we have more autistic children, yet we are not
> providing the special classrooms or the schools for
> these autistic children. When they are available, they
> are at a huge expense to parents. I think we need to
> take that into consideration. We need to look at this.
> It is no good saying that we have to allow these kids
> to feel good about themselves and that we do not
> want to upset them and make them feel hurt. I under-
> stand that, but we have to be realistic at times and
> consider the impact this is having on other children
> in the classroom.

Where do we start? Before the beginning?

No doubt, the Critical Discourse Analyst (CDA), the Disability Studies
in Education (DSE) scholar, the sociologist or the Human Rights lawyer
have much to work on with their readings of the extracts from Senator Hanson's speeches. The remarks are extremely clumsy and reveal ignorance
of, or disregard for, the linguistic, legal and political conventions that have
been established to avoid prejudice in the form of *ableism*. Lurking in her
remarks is what Sally Tomlinson describes as the discourse of *benevolent
humanitarianism*.[12] Ableism is concealed behind the cloak of "segregation
for their own good".

Disabled researchers and advocates have long argued that the way we
describe disability reflects our ontological disposition. Put simply, the way
we talk about disability reflects how we understand and, in turn, represent,
the nature and meaning of disability. These representations instantiate relations of power, relations of powerlessness. This is what Michael Oliver
established as *the politics of disablement*.[13] There are numerous accounts of
the misrepresentation and maltreatment of people with impairments, including genocide and incarceration, through time and place that provide practical lessons in the effects of ontology.[14]

Let us pursue this further. Disability is often described as a *personal tragedy* that befalls individuals as a consequence of their pathological *defects*
or impairments. Such an interpretation invites pity that elicits charitable
responses. We see this in the descriptions of these poor suffering people –
the disabled. This also extends to their families, it is so often said, who
must, when all is said and done, be grieving for the *normal* person their

child might have been. It is an oft repeated refrain in schools: *"They (the parents) just haven't accepted their child's disability"*.

Disability might also be described in purely medical or clinical terms. Disability is reduced to an inventory of symptoms that are indicative of defective pathologies. Our response then is to see the disabled person as *abnormal* and in need of medical intervention – diagnosis, treatment, management and if chance or science would have it – a cure. These understandings of disability – of disabled people – are individualistic. It is a personal tragedy, an individual event, because of the attributes or the defective impaired pathology of that person. There is a reductive process at work. The identity of the disabled person is seen solely in terms of their impairment. All of the other elements of their identity are rendered secondary, invisible and worthless. Looking into the film director's tool-bag, this is referred to as *mise-en-scène*. A French term, it means 'placing on stage'.

An alternative formulation for understanding and responding to disability is presented in what has come to be known and described as *the social model of disability*.[15] Here we apply C. Wright Mills' *sociological imagination*.[16] For Mills, problems that are often described as *personal troubles* are actually *social issues*. The representation of these social issues as personal troubles is what William Ryan calls *victim blaming*.[17] According to the social model of disability, disability is a description of a set of social relations rather than of individual pathology. Disablement is a function of the interactions between societies; its institutions, values and culture, and the differences presented by a range of human characteristics that do not conform to a standardised or ordained body type. Societies may more or less enable or disable its citizenry. Different societies erect barriers to access and participation in accordance with their own sets of norms. As Zygmunt Bauman observes, *all* societies create their own set of strangers in their own inimitable ways.[18] Herein our language is reoriented. Our analysis is directed towards the ways in which institutions can pursue structural and cultural adjustments to support inclusion. This framework is embraced by disability discrimination legislation and human rights conventions across international jurisdictions.

These descriptions do not exhaust the discursive frameworks that we see at play in the history of understanding, talking about and responding to impairment, disability and disablement. Nor do my representations extend to the nuances within them, or indeed to the debates within the disability movement about these models and platforms for research.[19] In this essay I am not venturing into different strands of disability studies to elaborate *Crip Studies, critical studies of ableism* or *disability studies of the global south*. The point here is to simply provide initial prompts for interrogating the language of Senator Hanson and the perspective she represents. Aided by these discursive prompts, let us now return to, Senator Hanson's remarks and reconsider the politics of disablement at work in her speeches about children with disabilities, including autism.

Her first utterance to her colleagues in the Senate chamber, although typically few of them were present to listen to her, on Wednesday, 21 June 2017, erects a binary of *normal classrooms* and *special classrooms*. It may be self-evident, but for the record let's be clear. The *normal classroom* is for children "*straining at the bit and wanting to get o*n", and the *special classroom* is for disabled and autistic children "*who take up the normal classroom teacher's time*", and who require "*special attention*" and "*need to be looked after*". There is an implied, if not overt, statement of differential expectation for the different groups of students. Aspirations are high for the students who should remain in the normal classroom. The language shifts from an educational lexicon to a discourse of care and treatment as we move from the *normal classroom* to the *special classroom* wherein children are to be "*looked after*".

The deployment of the unverifiable and provocative term *normal* establishes a hierarchy which privileges and includes most children, though it has to be said the membership of this club is surely dwindling as we witness the inexorable growth of classifications of disorder and impairment.[20] The options for the assignment of *special educational needs* and consignment to the *special classroom* have experienced what economists would describe as the multiplier effect thanks largely to the consolidation of the *Diagnostic and statistical manual of mental disorders (DSM)* as a quasi-educational aid.[21] Immediately, the *abnormal* child is *an additional child* whose rightful place, irrespective of the law and nation states' endorsements of international conventions,[22] is to be removed. Their removal is for their own good, for special attention, care and treatment. The benevolent humanitarianism at play in this division of children reflects a discourse of care and, inferentially, pity. The twist of the knife is that this time-honoured process of segregation is now widely described in the vernacular of inclusion. The site for children with disabilities is now the inclusion programme or inclusion centre.

It is also important to contest the often-repeated assertion that the disabled and autistic student is holding back the progress of others, the so-called *normal students*. Clearly, some of us need more time and/or support to grasp different concepts, to read printed text, to turn a page, to decipher and perform an algorithm, communicate an idea, negotiate conflict or disruption, get from one room to another, to throw a ball, or to undertake an examination. Supportive strategies, and other resources to render the lesson; both content and the teaching and learning activities, accessible are available. The teacher may need additional curriculum materials that instance a concept in various ways. They may require specific, sometimes very expensive, technologies to ensure access and participation; it may be Braille translations for students with vision impairments, it could be a purpose designed and built chair and table, it could also be a person performing sign language translation for children who cannot hear the teacher's instructions, it could be an additional teacher or assistant in the room to ensure that all children are managing to access and understand the lessons, it could be that additional time is required to complete a test or set of activities. In a relatively short period of time we have witnessed the development of new and reasonably inexpensive technologies to support accessibility to the school curriculum. These are reasonable accommodations as set out at law in the Disability Discrimination Act (1992) and stipulated by the Disability Standards in Education (2005). Incorporation of the principles of *Universal Design for Learning*[23] in classroom teaching mitigates the challenge of difference. I am mindful of Michael Oliver pointing out that humans can't fly, but decisions were made and invested directed to develop the technology to make this possible.

Research by Tom Hehir and his colleagues in the Harvard University Faculty of Law Disability Project, Mel Ainscow, Alan Dyson and Susie Miles at the University of Manchester, and Lani Florian, Martyn Rouse and Kristine Black-Hawkins at the Universities of Edinburgh and Cambridge supports the general claim that the adjustments made to classrooms, to curriculum and to pedagogy to render classrooms more inclusive and enabling also benefit students without disabilities.[24] That schools can build inclusive cultures, programmes and classrooms to promote better academic and social outcomes for all students has been widely documented both in individual school case studies and system-wide reviews.[25] The determination of Tony Booth to build dynamism and contingency into *The Index for Inclusion* is instructive for assisting schools and their communities to secure inclusion and improved quality in the education programme for all students.

Talking about *ableism* in education

The London-based journalist Reni Eddo-Lodge's book: *Why I'm no longer talking to white people about race*, is instructive for those wanting to grapple with and apprehend the workings of institutional prejudice such as racism, sexism, homophobia and ableism.[26] In her preface she draws from a blog she wrote in 2014:

> *I'm no longer engaging with white people on the topic of race. Not all white people, just the vast majority who refuse to accept the legitimacy of structural racism and its symptoms. I can no longer engage with the gulf of an emotional disconnect that white people display when a*

*person of colour articulates their experience. You can see their eyes
shut down and harden. It's like treacle is poured into their ears, blocking up their ear canals. It's like they can no longer hear us.*

I would suggest that this is not too distant from the feelings provoked in
many of the parents of children with disabilities I have spoken with over
the years. Many of the stories they tell of their interactions with some
education administrators, teachers, school principals, school administrative staff and support personnel such as guidance officers or psychologists
depict people with 'blocked ears and hardened hearts'. It is tragic enough
that their ears are blocked to the requests from parents. Worse still is the
fact they have been encouraged to refuse to listen to what the research on
inclusive education is telling them. Professional development workshops
dedicated to the recognition and elimination of structural ableism in education are overdue.

Returning to Eddo-Lodge, the disconnect is explained in terms of race
and whiteness:

*This emotional disconnect is the conclusion of living a life oblivious to
the fact that their skin colour is the norm and all others deviate from
it. At best, white people have been taught not to mention that people of
colour are 'different' in case it offends us. They truly believe that the
experiences of their life as a result of their skin colour can and should
be universal. I just can't engage with the bewilderment and the defen-
siveness as they try to grapple with the fact that not everyone experiences the world in the way that they do. They've never had to think
about what it means, in power terms, to be white, so any time they're
vaguely reminded of this fact, they interpret it as an affront. Their eyes
glaze over in boredom or widen in indignation. Their mouths start
twitching as they get defensive. Their throats open up as they try to
interrupt, itching to talk over you but not really to listen, because they
need to let you know that you've got it wrong.*

*The journey towards understanding structural racism still requires
people of colour to prioritise white feelings. Even if they can hear you,
they're not really listening. It's like something happens to the words as
they leave our mouths and reach their ears. The words hit a barrier of
denial and they don't get any further.*

*That's the emotional disconnect. It's not really surprising, because
they've never known what it means to embrace a person of colour
as a true equal, with thoughts and feelings that are as valid as their
own . . . .* **Who really wants to be alerted to a structural system that
benefits them at the expense of others?**[27]

Like racism, ableism presents barriers to the established rights of participation in civil society for people with disability. Drawing from the work
of Lennard Davis,[28] Susan Wendell[29] and Susan Gabel,[30] Dan Goodley
describes ableism as: "social biases against people whose bodies function
differently from those bodies considered to be 'normal' and beliefs and
practices resulting from and interacting with these biases to serve discrimination".[31] Recognising, acknowledging and dismantling ableism represents
the difficult first steps for inclusive education. We remain a long way away
from accomplishing this. As Stephanie Gotlib correctly identifies in her
opinion piece for the Australian Broadcasting Commission, Senator Hanson's remarks are but an expression of the common knowledge. We need
to expose that common knowledge for its ableist foundations. Let me try to
explain this more carefully by further examining an opinion piece written
by Professor Kenneth Wiltshire.

An emeritus professor of political science at the University of Queensland and Australia's representative on the executive board of UNESCO,
Kenneth Wiltshire sought to impose clarity on the debate provoked by Senator Pauline Hanson's statements in an opinion piece for *The Australian*
entitled *Special needs education calls for co-operative effort*.[32] Commencing with the sub-heading "Intellectual disabilities are more common than
ever and demand a renewed focus", Professor Wiltshire intones the voice
of reason. The claim of the exponential increase in the numbers of students
with intellectual disabilities is advanced without supporting evidence or
sufficient clarification about his terms of reference. He suggests that 12 per
cent of the total school population will have some form of intellectual disability. He applauds Catholic and independent schools that, unlike schools
in the state and territory jurisdictions, have the autonomy to apply flexible
responses such as special classes and the establishment of special schools
for autism. This fails to recognise that state schools all around Australia
have established, and not evaluated, special needs and inclusion classrooms
to which students with disabilities are consigned for part of or all of the
day. It does not observe the opening of new separate special schools and the
refurbishment of existing special schools by state and territory jurisdictions.
Nor does it consider the role of the Autism Hub in his home state of Queensland.[33] Make no mistake, special education flourishes in the state sector and
so-called independent sectors.

Professor Wiltshire is critical of government departments of health and
education silos that have eschewed cooperative research on this matter. Also
under fire are Faculties of Education that refuse to drill down *'beyond their
beloved first order research'* to second order research into causes rather than
trends. The opinion piece does not acknowledge the establishment of a major
government funded research initiative, the Cooperative Research Centre

for Living with Autism that partners his University of Queensland, Autism Queensland, Queensland University of Technology, Autism Spectrum Australia, Mater Research, Latrobe University, Curtin University, The University of Western Australia, the Queensland government, The University of New South Wales, Griffith University, and the AEIOU Foundation which is the world's first cooperative centre to research autism across the lifespan.

Professor Wiltshire rejects the *'con job'* of inclusive education as a cost-cutting measure and advances a tripartite approach calling for full-time inclusion for some students, partial inclusion for others with flexible provision of special classes staffed by trained teachers and aides, and special schools for others. This is, of course, Senator Hanson's recommendation.

It may appear fitting that, as Australia's representative on the executive board of UNESCO he invokes the *Salamanca Statement and Framework for Action on Special Needs Education* to advance this agenda. The Salamanca Statement, notwithstanding the ambivalence of its historical moment in June 1994, is not advancing an extension of special education, as does Professor Wiltshire. It states that: *"regular schools with this inclusive orientation are the most effective means of combating discriminatory attitudes, creating welcoming communities, building an inclusive society and achieving education for all; moreover, they provide an effective education to the majority of children and improve the efficiency and ultimately the cost-effectiveness of the entire education system".*[34] Perhaps UNESCO is the source of the 'con job'? The passage of time has secured international firmament around the establishment of the regular school as the site for the education of children with disabilities.[35] Article 24 of the United Nations Convention on the Rights of Persons with Disabilities (2006) to which Australia is one of the 160 signatories, is clear about the right and the appropriateness of the regular school and classroom as the site for the education of all students. It is useful to look at the provisions of Article 24, for it is often cited and expected that we are familiar with its contents.

2   *In realizing this right, States Parties shall ensure that:*

  (a) *Persons with disabilities are not excluded from the general education system on the basis of disability, and that children with disabilities are not excluded from free and compulsory primary education, or from secondary education, on the basis of disability;*
  (b) *Persons with disabilities can access an inclusive, quality and free primary education and secondary education on an equal basis with others in the communities in which they live;*
  (c) *Reasonable accommodation of the individual's requirements is provided;*

(d) *Persons with disabilities receive the support required, within the general education system, to facilitate their effective education;*

(e) *Effective individualized support measures are provided in environments that maximize academic and social development, consistent with the goal of full inclusion.*[36]

Professor Wiltshire, having not checked on research being undertaken in his own university, hasn't ventured further afield to the work of respected academics around the world who demonstrate the shortcomings of separate special schooling and the benefits of inclusive education. Here I refer not only to the aforementioned research from Harvard University and the Universities of Manchester, Edinburgh and Cambridge, but more particularly to recent reviews of education for students with disabilities in Australian education jurisdictions.[37]

Wiltshire calls for appropriately funded schooling. On this point both he and Senator Hanson are correct. Building the capacity of Australian schools to educate all children requires funding for infrastructure reforms, changes to curriculum and assessment and innovations to the understanding of teaching and learning. The challenge here is not simply returning to the Treasury cap in hand to ask for additional funds. The challenge is how you build the capacity of a system to be able to provide all children with an inclusive and excellent educational experience. Segregation is costly. It draws heavily from the public purse, not to mention personal costs that are accrued. Bifurcated systems are expensive. Segregation leads to exclusion and underachievement that will be paid for later through the juvenile and adult criminal justice systems, through social welfare dependency and the health system.

Let's be clear. Professor Wiltshire and Senator Hanson are saying much the same thing. Professor Wiltshire has had many more years of finishing school than did Senator Hanson so his language is more conciliatory, and seemingly more authoritative and correct. Nevertheless, it is profoundly ableist. It amounts to much the same – students with disabilities despite their standing before the law cannot assume that their right to be in the neighbourhood school is guaranteed. This state of affairs is achieved through the saturation of our discourse and thinking with the quasi-medical posturing of *special educational needs*. The conceptual foundations and usage of terms like *special educational needs* passes without a second thought. *Special education needs* must be attended to by special teachers and aides and preferably in special classrooms and schools. It is as if the word special is an irrefutable scientific descriptor, the mention of which is sufficient to trigger particular ways of dealing with children and adults with disabilities.

Special has become a marker of position on the educational hierarchy. Students without disabilities are the first comers. Decisions about students with disabilities are a second-order concern. Testing this claim might be well served by considering the reactions of education jurisdictions, of the community and of educators in general to the routine redirection of students from one school to another because of their disability and the assumed difficulties that this might cause. Jurisdictions are aware that this happens. Public schools routinely redefine "public". In focus groups, I have been appalled at hearing educators refer to students with disabilities as *additional students*. This is the Hanson and Wiltshire inference. It is, though the protagonists would be shocked to hear it, ableism. There is a reticence amongst many parents to raise issues about the experiences of their children with disabilities with their respective schools for fear of worsening the situation and being forced to opt for a segregated school.

Meanwhile back at the swimming pool

I attended a conference on inclusive education hosted by a progressive teachers' union. I say this because teachers' unions have stood in opposition to inclusive education, seeing it as a threat to the industrial conditions of their members. Thankfully this has changed over time for many, though not all, teachers' professional associations. There were many highlights at the conference. Presentations by children, by teachers, school principals, parents and school governors reflected the determination of some school communities to build community by making their school engaging for all children. The conference also crystallised the enduring problem of continuing to think in terms of special and regular education. Let me explain.

A group of principals from special schools described their adoption of inclusive education. Ah, you say, they dispersed their resources and children to local community schools, drew the curtains and locked the doors. I'm afraid not. This had been achieved by maintaining their base operation – separate schools for students with disabilities – and also by forming a cluster with a group of regular schools to provide expert Special Educational Needs services such as through a "Super SENCO" who could service the cluster. If it quacks like a duck, as the saying goes, it's still special education. This is not the kind of reform of both special and regular schooling that is required to ensure an inclusive education for all students. It deepens the relations of exclusion.

It seemed to me that the special school folk had gone to the ladder of the high diving board. Had a discussion at the bottom and bravely scaled the ladder. Walking out to the end of the board, they had looked below them at the vast and unfamiliar possibilities beneath and shuffled back down the ladder to firm and familiar territory. The pity is that we could all draw from the well of courage and be "*diving for pearls*".

Notes

1 I draw the title for this essay from Elvis Costello's poignant protest against the Falklands war in the song 'Shipbuilding': in that he says that "we're diving for dear life, when we could be diving for pearls".

2 "A Remark You Made" track 2, side 1 Heavy Weather, composed by Joe Zawinul, 1977. Heavy Weather reached number 1 on the US jazz album charts, 33 on the R&B charts and 30 on Billboard 200. In 2011 the album was inducted into the Grammy Hall of Fame.

3 For a critical review of Pauline Hanson and the One Nation Party read Richard Cooke (2017) ALT-WRONG: the incoherence of the Australian right. *The Monthly*, April, pages 20–25; David Marr (2017) The White Queen: one nation and the politics of race. *Quarterly Essay*, 65: 1–102.

4 Matthew Killoran. (2017) Pauline Hanson says that Autistic Kids should be removed from the mainstream classroom. *The Courier Mail*, Brisbane, June 21st 2017 6.55pm. www.couriermail.com.au/news/queensland/pauline-hanson-says-autistic-kids-should-be-removed-from-mainstream-classes/news-story/9aca507 ace3efc707dfa0d7648fc6180 (Retrieved June 25th 2017 1.10 pm).

5 Karen Barlow. (2017) Emma Husar hits back at Pauline Hanson's 'Uneducated' comments about Autism in schools – the one nation leader is under fire for suggesting autistic children be segregated. *The Huffington Post Australia*, June 22nd 2017 2.15 PM AEST. www.huffingtonpost.com.au/2017/06/21/emma-husar-hits-back-at-pauline-hansons-uneducated-comments-a_a_22533376/ (Retrieved June 25th 2017 2.10 pm AEST).

6 Senate Hansard. (2017) Questions without notice. *Parliament of Australia*, Canberra, Thursday, June 22nd 2017, page 48.

7 Education Minister Senator Birmingham's refusal to repudiate the remarks of Senator Hanson is a direct reflection of the balance of power in Australian Federal politics where the government relies on the minority parties and independent members for support to pass its programme of legislation.

8 Waleed Aly quoted in "Waleed Aly explains what it's like raising a child with autism", *News.com.au*, June 23rd 2017 01:57 AEST. www.news.com.au/entertainment/tv/radio/waleed-aly-explains-what-pauline-hanson-doesnt-understand-about-autism/news-story/fe78b30305f0d7b42a0938f88988a989 (Retrieved June 26th 2017 07.15 AEST).

9 Gotlib, S. (2017) Opinion Piece: Gonski 2.0: Pauline Hanson's insensitive remarks aren't the only bad news for disabled students. *ABC News*, Melbourne, Thursday June 22nd 17:52 AEST. www.abc.net.au/news/2017-06-22/gonski-pauline-hanson-remarks-not-only-bad-news/8643208 (Retrieved June 27th 2017 02:43 AEST). Gonski 2.0 is a reference to the author of the federal review of funding for Australian schools, David Gonski. The Review was commissioned by a Labor government and then rejected by a successive Liberal government. Gonski 2:0 refers to a revised version of the model suggested by David Gonski. The Gonski Report is etched into the Australian political landscape now and is a major focus for Australian Education Union campaigns.

10 Here I am mindful of Ellen Brantlinger's careful application of Mick Dunkin's rules of research to an analysis of the critique leveled at inclusive education researchers by traditional special education researchers such as James Kauffman and Daniel Hallahan. The charge by Kauffman is that inclusive education is ideological and therefore incapable of being regarded as scientific. This is of

course an old debate applied to a different field. Earlier Martyn Hammersley and Roger Gomm had leveled the same critique at the anti-racist education research of Barry Troyna. In speaking with Julie Allan, Deborah Youdell and I, David Gillborn incisively observes that ideology is like sweat; "you smell everyone's but your own". See: Brantlinger, E. A. (1997) Using ideology: Cases of non-recognition of the politics of research and practice in special education. *Review of Educational Research*, 67(4): 425–459; Kauffman, J. M. and D. P. Hallahan (1995) *The illusion of full inclusion: a comprehensive critique of a current special education bandwagon*. Austin, TX: Pro-Ed; Dunkin, M. J. (1996) Types of errors in synthesizing research in education. *Review of Educational Research*, 66(1): 87–97; Allan, J. and Slee, R. (2008) *Doing inclusive education research*. Rotterdam: Sense Publishers.

11 Senator Pauline Hanson (2017) The Senate Hansard, Canberra. *The Parliament of Australia*, Thursday June 22nd 2017, page 99.

12 Tomlinson, S. (1982) *A sociology of special education*. London: Routledge & Kegan Paul. Sally revised this seminal work and it was published by Routledge (2017) under the title of A sociology of special and inclusive education: the manufacturing of inability.

13 Oliver, M. (1990) *The politics of disablement*. Basingstoke: Palgrave Macmillan.

14 A representative illustration of this work should include but not be limited to: Stiker, H-J. (1999) *A history of disability*. Ann Arbor, MI: University of Michigan Press; Snyder, S. L. and Mitchell, D. T. (2006) *Cultural locations of disability*. Chicago: University of Chicago Press; Mitchell, D. T. and Snyder, S. L. (1997) *The body and physical difference: discourses of disability*. Ann Arbor, MI: University of Michigan Press; Nussbaum, M. C. (2004) *Hiding from humanity: disgust, shame, and the law*. Princeton, NJ: Princeton University Press; Nussbaum, M. C. (2006) *Frontiers of justice: disability, nationality, species membership*. Cambridge, MA: The Belknap Press of Harvard University Press; Bogdan, R. (1988) *Freak show: presenting human oddities for amusement and profit*. Chicago: University of Chicago Press; Foucault, M. (1965) *Madness and civilization: a history of insanity in the age of reason*. New York: Vintage, 1988.

15 Oliver, M. (2009) *Understanding disability: from theory to practice*. Basingstoke: Palgrave Macmillan.

16 Wright Mills, C. (1959) *The sociological imagination*. New York: Oxford University Press.

17 Ryan, W. P. (1971) *Blaming the victim*. London: Orbach & Chambers.

18 Bauman, Z. (1997) *Postmodernity and its discontents*. Cambridge: Polity.

19 See for example: Shakespeare, T. (2006) *Disability rights and wrongs*. London: Routledge; Oliver, M. and Barnes, C. (2012) *The new politics of disablement*. Basingstoke: Palgrave Macmillan; Goodley, D., Hughes, B. and Davis, L. (2012) *Disability and social theory: new developments and directions*. Basingstoke: Palgrave Macmillan.

20 See for example: Goodley, D. (2017) *Disability studies: an interdisciplinary introduction*. London: Sage; Davis, L. J. (2013) *The end of normal: identity in a biocultural era*. Ann Arbor, MI: University of Michigan Press; Titchkosky, T. (2007) *Reading and writing disability differently: the textured life of embodiment*. Toronto: University of Toronto Press.

21 American Psychiatric Association (2013) *Diagnostic and statistical manual of mental disorders: DSM-5*. Arlington, VA: American Psychiatric Association.

Tobin, R. M. and House, A. E. (2016) *DSM-5 diagnosis in the schools.* New York: Guildford Press.

22 Let us not forget that Australia is a signatory to the United Nations Conventions on the Rights of Persons with Disability [UNCRPD] (2006) and that Australian schools are bound by the provisions of the Disability Discrimination Act [DDA] (1992) and the Disability Standards in Education [DSE] (2005) that proceed from the DDA. UNCRPD binds its 161 signatory states to ensure that "persons with disabilities can access an inclusive, quality and free primary education and secondary education on an equal basis with others in the communities in which they live." Article 24 of the convention binds its signatories to ensure an inclusive education system at all levels for people with disabilities as well as opportunities for life-long learning. Article 24 requires that students with disabilities must not be excluded from general education, that reasonable accommodations and individualized supports must be provided for them, and that people with disabilities should have access to tertiary education, vocational training, and adult education on an equal basis with non-disabled students.

23 Hall, T. E., et al. (Eds.) (2012) *Universal design for learning in the classroom.* New York: Guildford Press.

24 Florian, L., Rouse, L. and Black-Hawkins, K. (2017) *Achievement and inclusion in schools.* London: Routledge; Farrell, P., Dyson, A., Polat, F., Hutcheson, G., and Gallannaugh, F. (2007) Inclusion and achievement in mainstream schools. *European Journal of Special Needs Education,* 22(2): 131–145. http://doi. org/10.1080/08856250701267808; Dessemontet, R. S., & Bless, G. (2013) The impact of including children with intellectual disability in general education classrooms on the academic achievement of their low-, average-, and high-achieving peers. *Journal of Intellectual and Developmental Disability,* 38(1): 23–30. http://doi.org/10.3 109/13668250.2012.757589; Hehir, T., Grindal, T., Freeman, B., Lamoreau, R., Borquaye, Y. and Burke, S. (2016) *A summary of evidence on inclusive education.* Sao Paulo: Instituto Alana.

25 Henderson, B. (2011) *The blind advantage: how going blind made me a stronger principal and how including children with disabilities made our school better for everyone.* Cambridge, MA: Harvard Educational Press.

26 Eddo-Lodge, R. (2017) *Why I'm no longer talking to White people about race.* London: Bloomsbury Circus.

27 Ibid., pages i–xi. (my emphasis).

28 Davis, L. J. (2013) *The end of normal. Identity in a biocultural era.* Ann Arbor, MI: University of Michigan Press.

29 Wendell, S. (1996) *The rejected body: feminist philosophical reflections on disability.* New York: Routledge.

30 Gabel, S. (2006) *Disability studies and inclusive education: negotiating tensions and integrating research, policy and practice.* Paper presented at 2nd International City Conference of Disability Studies on Disability Studies in Education, Michigan State University.

31 Goodley, D. (2011) *Disability studies: an interdisciplinary introduction.* Los Angeles: Sage.

32 Wiltshire, K. (2017) Special needs education calls for cooperative effort. *Commentary, The Australian,* Sydney, Newscorp., July 1–2, page 22.

33 https://ahrc.eq.edu.au.

34 UNESCO (1994) *The Salamanca statement and framework for action on special needs education.* Geneva: United Nations Educational, Scientific and Cultural

Organisation, Madrid, Ministry of Education and Science Spain, Salamanca, Spain, 7–10 June, ix, http://unesdoc.unesco.org/images/0009/000984/098427eo. pdf (Retrieved July 3rd 2017 10:17 AEST).

35 The European Agency on Special Needs and Inclusive Education (2017) *The agency's position on inclusive education systems*. Brussels. www.european-agency.org/about-us/who-we-are/position-on-inclusive-education-systems (Retrieved July 3rd 2017 10:29 AEST).

36 United Nations (2006) *United Nations Convention on the Rights of Persons with Disabilities and Optional Protocol (UNCRPD)*, New York. www.un.org/disabilities/documents/convention/convoptprot-e.pdf (Retrieved July 3rd 2017 1042 AEST).

37 For example: Deloitte Access Economics (2017) *Review of education for students with disability in Queensland state schools*. Brisbane: Department of Education and Training. http://education.qld.gov.au/schools/disability/docs/disability-review-report.pdf (Retrieved July 3rd 2017 15.04 AEST); Victoria Department of Education and Training (2016) *Review of the program for students with disabilities*. Melbourne: DET. www.education.vic.gov.au/Docu ments/about/department/PSD-Review-Report.pdf (Retrieved July 3rd 2017 15.09 AEST). Shaddock, A., Packer, S. and Roy, A. (2015) *Schools for all children and young people: report of the expert panel on students with complex needs and challenging behaviour*. Canberra: Australian Capital Territory Department for Education.

Interlude

The Blind Man with the Lamp

It was night and I had made the greatest decision of the century –
I would save humanity – but how? – as thousands of thoughts were
tormenting me I heard footsteps, opened the door and beheld the blind
man from the opposite room walking down the hallway and holding
a lamp – he was about to go down the stairs – 'What is he doing with
the lamp?', I asked myself and suddenly an idea flashed through my

mind – I found the answer – 'My dear brother', I said to him, 'God has sent you',

And with zeal we both got down to work . . .

An extract from Tasos Leivaditis (2014) *The Blind Man with the Lamp*, (Translated and Introduced by N.N. Trakakis), Limni, Evia, Greece, Denise Harvey Publisher.

Coda
The man, the fountain and the struggle for existence

Browsing my way through the book exhibitors' tables at the European Conference on Educational Research in Copenhagen last year, I was stopped in my tracks by a title on the Routledge table: *Inclusion is Dead. Long Live Inclusion.* The absence of information about its contents on the back outside cover witheld clues about its contents. Purchasing the last copy on display, I found a chair nearby, set my bag down beside me and commenced reading. To their credit, the authors Peter Imray and Andrew Colley stake their claim at the outset:

> *The fundamental premise of this book is that educational inclusion, despite a constantly changing and liquid definition, has not been achieved in any country under any educational system despite some 30 years of trying. It was no doubt a valiant and laudable attempt to ensure justice and equity but its failure must now be addressed. Inclusion has become a recurring trope of academic writing on education; it is trotted out as an eternal and unarguable truth, but it is neither. It doesn't work, and it never has worked. Inclusion is dead.*[1]

To be sure, in some quarters inclusive education has had the life sucked out of it. Again, we return to Edward Said's dictum about travelling theories losing their insurrectionary zeal as they are popularised. They are, he says, *"tamed and domesticated"*.[2] *"When I look at the world"*,[3] democracy too has its feet up in the air – corrupted as it is by the global populist surges of the far right. Still, let us not walk away from democracy or inclusive education just yet. Both are worth fighting for. They have a basis in principles that retain utility for a troubled and troubling world. They, democracy and inclusive education, are of course linked. Bernstein[4] identifies inclusion as a prerequisite for a democratic education. As was his way, he pursues precision by stipulating that inclusion is not a simile for absorption, it is not assimilation. Imray and Colley could apply a more careful analysis before arriving at their diagnosis and withdrawing life support. As Jody Carr, a Minister in the government of the province of New Brunswick in Canada, stated at an inclusive education conference in Sydney recently, "*When people tell me inclusive education doesn't work, I tell them that that's because it's not inclusive education*".

As inclusive education began to gather momentum through adoption, more or less, by organisations such as UNESCO and the OECD and found expression in the policy statements of jurisdictions around the world, special educators rebranded themselves. Definitions were struck to suit interests. Not surprisingly the contradictions and tensions became apparent. It remains my view that special and regular educators who have resisted fundamental changes to the structures and cultures of education have corrupted the reforming spirit of inclusive education. Just as democracy is not an expression of laissez-faire political and social organisation, demanding as it does civic conventions based on rights and responsibilities, inclusive education is a call for a reformulation of schooling wherein "special" and "regular" are jettisoned and the segregation of students with disabilities is seen as a relic of a bygone age. Foundational principles of non-segregation, access, representation, participation and success are unconditional for inclusive educators. There are jurisdictions around the world where inclusive education is vibrant and leading system reform. Moreover, there are schools and communities whose commitment to inclusive education for all comers has been successful. They provide a model and a catalytic force for others interested in the fundamental reforms required for schools to diminish exclusion.

Other people's wishes

Wander down to the end of Grafton Street in Dublin and you will find an oasis in a bustling city that is St Stephen's Green. Having walked from Croke Park passing both the Irish Writer's Museum in Parnell Square and the Dublin City Gallery, The Hugh Lane and then through the shopping precinct, the lush gardens and park benches offered the respite I craved. It was a blue-sky, bold-sun autumn lunchtime. Don't be fooled. Still, it was very cool, very crisp. People wore coats, others added scarves and gloves. Parents or minders walked to the water's edge, their children's hands held tightly as they coaxed them to see all the different species of water birds whose home St Stephen's Green is. City workers and school children sat talking and eating their lunches. Ubiquitous Lycra-cladded city joggers rushed through the Green, their eyes fixed to the distance or to their Fitbit, all the while checking their step and distance counts, as well as keeping an eye on their heart rates lest it stopped. Others strolled pushing prams;

behind them shuffled folk with sticks or walking frames. There were dogs, even a 'Westie' (West Highland Terrier) that made me think of Poppy back home, on and off their leads following their noses, checking their pee-mail. I had happened on a pastoral scene in the city centre.

Blake's reveries of innocence gave way to blasts of experience in the form of a fountain in the centre of the Green. The fountain also serves as a wishing well. People no doubt toss their coins and wish for better times in love, health, prosperity, football – who knows what. A lone figure was perched on the side of this wishing well, his arm reaching down for the coins. The water would no doubt be very cold and he was stretching and progressively saturating his arm, shoulder and then he climbed in to gather more coins. As he came out of the well, I surmised that this was a homeless man, as he seemed to be wearing many layers and he retrieved a bunch of plastic bags in which he carried his belongings. I wrote in my notebook, to capture the moment, *"the homeless man gathers other people's wishes"*. In truth, I had crossed out "steals" and opted for the gentler "gathers". After all, people had discarded their coins to secure their wishes – who owns the coins then?

The image of the drenched homeless man with his fistful of coins and scooped-up wishes returned to me as I sat in a room on the other side of the world listening to a group of parents of children with disabilities speaking of the experiences of their children for whom they tried to secure an inclusive education. They speak with the quiet despair and suppressed anger that comes from the heartbreak they feel. Stories piled up of principals, guidance officers, school office managers and teachers telling them to find a more suitable school; the regular school in the next suburb or the special school for children *"just like theirs"*. I heard about the various arrangements made for children to attend for part of the school day or part of the week. They spoke of their children spending most of their time with the adult teacher's aide or in a room called the inclusion room, the special needs room or the enrichment room, which was not uncommon; of children having separate supervised recess and lunch breaks; of children not being able to go on their class excursion; of parents paying for additional support in the school; of children not having the opportunity to make friendships with other children – always having adults with them; of parents not speaking out because they might upset the teacher or the school principal and lose the place in the school; and finally of parents giving up and going to the special school. The CEO of *Inclusion Alberta*, Bruce Uditsky, is unequivocal. When a teacher tells him that the child with the disability should not be included in the local school, he says: *"You just broke those parents' hearts"*.

Parents told me of opting for a special school because their child would not be bullied, their child would be cared for or that there would be the resources available to ensure that they were learning. This is perfectly understandable. But for me it begs the questions:

- Why aren't neighbourhood schools free from bullying?
- Why aren't some children cared about in the neighbourhood school?
- Why aren't the resources for all children's education available in the neighbourhood school?

Is it unreasonable to assume that all schools be places free from bullying; places where all children are valued and instilled with a sense of belonging and value; places where a quality education is provided for all? This is so often bound up in the rhetoric of choice and then wrapped tightly in the scientific claims of special education. Catia Malaquias exposes three common myths of special education:

- Your child has special needs.
- Children with special needs do better in "specialist" settings.
- Special schools are needed – and parents need to be able to choose them – because one size does not fit all.[5]

Parents should be able to choose a separate special school if they so wish – we are told. Let's be clear, there is no choice if going to the local school is untenable. It seems to me that parents of children with disabilities like the man at the fountain in Dublin are simply seeking other people's wishes – a good-quality education at the local school for their child with his or her neighbours and brothers and sisters. Since we have been wandering in Ireland, though not in Belfast, perhaps Van Morrison can help us to reorder our priorities, to eschew the neoliberal template for a good life for a few and a struggle for the rest. He suggests that if we could let our *hearts do the thinking* and let our *heads begin to feel*, then we'll *look upon the world anew*. Then we might have a way of detecting what is real, detecting what counts.[6] Make no mistake, this should not be dismissed as sentimentalism gone mad. The fact is that in an age of hyper-rationality, the world is unhinged and we have strayed from principles of community and inclusion.

My grandchildren deserve a better education than their parents had. I want them to share the classroom with refugee children so that they will learn of the pain and futility of conflict. They deserve to rub shoulders with children from diverse ethnic, religious, linguistic and cultural backgrounds. They should not be condemned to learn about disability by periodic class visits to special schools as part of some liberal social service programme that softens the edges of an otherwise brutal curriculum. Our children and grandchildren deserve an education about and for humanity in humanity.

Inclusive education is a tactic we deploy in the pursuit of this democratic ideal.

Notes

1 Imray, P. and Colley, A. (2017) *Inclusion is dead: long live inclusion*. Abingdon: Routledge, page 1.
2 Said, E. W. (2000) Travelling theory reconsidered. In *Reflections on exile and other literary and cultural essays*. London: Granta Publications, pages 436–452.
3 Apologies to Lucinda Williams for borrowing the title of one her more sanguine compositions: When I Look at the World track 3, Disc 2 on the 2014 album: "Down where the Spirit Meets the Bone".
4 Bernstein, B. (1996) *Pedagogy, symbolic control and identity: theory, research, critique*. London: Taylor & Francis.
5 Malaquias, C. (2017) Three myths of special education – thoughts for parents, *Starting with Julius Organisation*, December 27th, www.startingwithjulius.org.au/3-myths-of-special-education-thoughts-for-parents/ (Retrieved February 2nd 2018 12:55 am AEDT).
6 Morrison, V. (2014) *I forgot that love existed: from lit up inside*. Edited by Eamonn Hughes. London: Faber & Faber, page 122.

References

Ainscow, M. (2007). Towards a more inclusive education system: where next for special schools? In R. Cigman (Ed.) *Included or excluded? The challenge of the mainstream for some SEN children*. London: Routledge, pages 128–139.

Ainscow, M. (2016). *Struggles for equity in education: the selected works of Mel Ainscow*. Abingdon: Routledge.

Allan, J. and Slee, R. (2008). *Doing inclusive education research*. Rotterdam: Sense Publishers.

Aly, W. (2017). Waleed Aly explains what it's like raising a child with autism. *News. com.au*, June 23rd 2017 01:57 AEST. www.news.com.au/entertainment/tv/radio/ waleed-aly-explains-what-pauline-hanson-doesnt-understand-about-autism/news-story/fe78b30305f0d7b42a0938f88988a989 (Retrieved June 26th 2017 07.15 AEST).

American Psychiatric Association (2013). *Diagnostic and statistical manual of mental disorders: DSM-5*. Arlington, VA: American Psychiatric Association.

Apple, M. W. (2001). *Educating the "right" way: markets, standards, God, and inequality*. London: Routledge Falmer.

Atkinson, A. B. (2015). *Inequality: what can be done?* Cambridge, MA: Harvard University Press.

Ball, S. J. (2007). *Education plc*. London: Routledge.

Ball, S. J. (2013). *Foucault, power, and education*. New York: Routledge.

Barlow, K. (2017). Emma Husar hits back at Pauline Hanson's 'Uneducated' comments about autism in schools – the one nation leader is under fire for suggesting autistic children be segregated. *The Huffington Post Australia*, June 22nd 2017, 2.15 PM AEST. www.huffingtonpost.com.au/2017/06/21/emma-husar-hits-back-at-pauline-hansons-uneducated-comments-a_a_22533376/ (Retrieved June 25th 2017 2.10 pm AEST)

Barton, L. and Landman, M. (1993). The politics of integration: observations on the warnock report. In R. Slee (Ed.) *Is there a desk with my name on it?* Lewes: Falmer Press.

Bauman, Z. (1997). *Postmodernity and its discontents*. Cambridge: Polity.

Bauman, Z. (2004). *Wasted lives: modernity and its outcasts*. Oxford: Polity.

Bauman, Z. (2008) Does ethics have a chance in a world of consumers? Cambridge, MA: Harvard University Press.

Bauman, Z. (2013). *Does the richness of the few benefit us all?* Cambridge: Polity.

Bauman, Z. (2016). *Strangers at my door*. Cambridge: Polity.

Beck, U. (2016). *The metamorphosis of the world*. Cambridge: Polity.

Berger, J. (1966). Lowry and the industrial north. In J. Berger (Ed.) (1980). *About looking*, London: Bloomsbury, pages 94–102.

Bernstein, B. (1996). *Pedagogy, symbolic control and identity: theory, research, critique*. London: Taylor & Francis.

Black-Hawkins, K., Florian, L., and Rouse, M. (2017). *Achievement and inclusion in schools*. Abingdon: Routledge.

Bogdan, R. (1988). *Freak show: presenting human oddities for amusement and profit*. Chicago: University of Chicago Press.

Bonneuil, C. and Fressoz, J.-B. (2017). *The shock of the anthropocene*. London: Verso.

Bourdieu, P. (2014). *On the state: lectures at the Collège de France, 1989–1992*. Cambridge: Polity.

Boyle, C., Anderson, J., and Swayn, N. (2015). Australia lags behind the evidence on special schools. *The Conversation*, August 5th 05.35 AEST. https://theconversa tion.com/australia-lags-behind-the-evidence-on-special-schools-41343 (Retrieved July 7th 2017 13.55 AEST).

Brantlinger, E. A. (1997). Using ideology: cases of nonrecognition of the politics of research and practice in special education. *Review of Educational Research*, 67(4): 425–459.

Brennan, B. (2017). *A writing life: Helen Garner and her work*. Melbourne: The Text Publishing Company.

Burt, C. (1937). *The backward child*. London: University of London Press.

Camus, J-Y. and Lebourg, N. (2017). *Far-right politics in Europe*. London: The Belknap Press of Harvard University Press.

Connolly, K. (2018). Use of sand vests to calm children with ADHD sparks controversy in Germany. *The Guardian*, London, January 20th.

Cooke, R. (2017). ALT-WRONG: the incoherence of the Australian right. *The Monthly*, April, pages 20–25.

Danforth, S. (2009). *The incomplete child: an intellectual history of learning disabilities*. New York: Peter Lang.

Davis, L. J. (2013). *The end of normal: identity in a biocultural era*. Ann Arbor, MI: The University of Michigan Press.

Deloitte Access Economics (2017). *Review of education for students with disability in Queensland state schools*. Brisbane: Department of Education and Training. http://education.qld.gov.au/schools/disability/docs/disability-review-report.pdf (Retrieved July 3rd 2017 15.04 AEST).

Department of Education and Science (1978). *Special educational needs: report of the committee of enquiry into the education of handicapped children and young people (Warnock Report)*. London: Her Majesty's Stationery Office.

Dessemontet, R. S. and Bless, G. (2013). The impact of including children with intellectual disability in general education classrooms on the academic achievement of their low-, average-, and high- achieving peers. *Journal of Intellectual*

and Developmental Disability, 38(1): 23–30. http://doi.org/10.3109/13668250.2
012.757589

Dorling, D. (2013). *The 32 stops: the central line*. London: Penguin.

Dorling, D. (2014). *Inequality and the 1%*. London: Verso.

Dunkin, M. J. (1996). Types of errors in synthesizing research in education. *Review of Educational Research*, 66(1): 87–97.

Dyson, A. and Kozleski, E. B. (2008). Disproportionality in special education – a transatlantic phenomenon. In L. Florian and M. J. McLaughlin (Eds.) *Disability classifications in education: issues and perspectives*. Thousand Oaks, CA: Corwin Press, pages 170–190.

The Economist (2012). *Briefings: in need of help*, November 10th–16th, pages 23–25.

Eddo-Lodge, R. (2017). *Why I'm no longer talking to white people about race*. London: Bloomsbury Circus.

European Agency on Special Needs and Inclusive Education (2017). *The agency's position on inclusive education systems*. Brussels: EASNIE. www.european-agency.org/about-us/who-we-are/position-on-inclusive-education-systems (Retrieved July 3rd 2017 10:29 AEST).

Fairclough, N. (2000). *New labour, new language*. London: Routledge.

Farrell, M. (2006). *Celebrating the special school*. London: David Fulton.

Farrell, P., Dyson, A., Polat, F., Hutcheson, G., and Gallannaugh, F. (2007). Inclusion and achievement in mainstream schools. *European Journal of Special Needs Education*, 22(2): 131–145. http://doi. org/10.1080/08856250701267808

Fleck, L. (1979). *Genesis and development of a scientific fact*. Chicago: University of Chicago Press.

Florian, L., Rouse, L., and Black-Hawkins, K. (2017). *Achievement and inclusion in schools*. London: Routledge.

Foucault, M. (1965). *Madness and civilization: a history of insanity in the age of reason*. New York: Vintage.

Frances, A. (2013). *Saving normal: an insider's revolt against out-of-control psychiatric diagnosis, DSM-5, Big Pharma, and the medicalization of ordinary life*. New York: William Morrow.

Gabel, S. (2006). *Disability studies and inclusive education: negotiating tensions and integrating research, policy and practice*. Paper presented at 2nd International City Conference of Disability Studies on Disability Studies in Education, Michigan State University.

Garner, H. (1996). Aqua Profonda. In H. Garner (Ed.) *True stories*. Melbourne: Text Publishing Melbourne, pages 223–228.

Gennari, J. (2016). *Blowin' hot and cool: Jazz and its critics*. Chicago: University of Chicago Press.

Gillborn, D. (2008). *Racism and education: coincidence or conspiracy?* London: Routledge.

Goodley, D. (2011). *Disability studies: an interdisciplinary introduction*. London: Sage.

Goodley, D. (2017). *Disability studies: an interdisciplinary introduction* (Second Edition). London: Sage.

Goodley, D., Hughes, B., and Davis, L. (2012). *Disability and social theory: new developments and directions*. Basingstoke: Palgrave Macmillan.

Gotlib, S. (2017). Opinion Piece: Gonski 2.0: Pauline Hanson's insensitive remarks aren't the only bad news for disabled students. *ABC News*, Melbourne, Thursday June 22nd 17:52 AEST. www.abc.net.au/news/2017-06-22/gonski-pauline-hanson-remarks-not-only-bad-news/8643208 (Retrieved June 27th 2017 02:43 AEST).

Hahn, H. (1987). Civil rights for disabled Americans: the foundation of a political agenda. In A. Gartner and T. Joe (Eds.) *Images of the disabled, disabling images*. New York: Praeger.

Hall, T. E., Meyer, A., and Rose, D. H. (Eds.) (2012). *Universal design for learning in the classroom*. New York: Guildford Press.

Hanson, P. (2017). The Senate Hansard, Canberra. *The Parliament of Australia*, Thursday June 22nd: 99.

Harry, B. (2014). The disproportionate placement of ethnic minorities in special education. In L. Florian (Ed.) *The Sage handbook of special education*. London: Sage, volume 1, pages 73–95.

Harvey, D. (1996). *Justice, nature, and the geography of difference*. Cambridge, MA: Blackwell Publishers.

Hehir, T., Grindal, T., Freeman, B., Lamoreau, R., Borquaye, Y., and Burke, S. (2016). *A summary of evidence on inclusive education*. Sao Paulo: Instituto Alana.

Hehir, T. and Katzman, L. I. (2012). *Effective inclusive schools: designing successful school-wide programs*. San Francisco: Jossey-Bass.

Hehir, T. and Schifter, L. A. (2015). *How did you get here? Students with disabilities and their journeys to Harvard*. Cambridge, MA: Harvard University Press.

Henderson, B. (2011). *The blind advantage: how going blind made me a stronger principal and how including children with disabilities made our school better for everyone*. Cambridge, MA: Harvard Educational Press.

Herrnstein, R. J. and Murray, C. A. (1994). *The bell curve: intelligence and class structure in American life*. London: Simon & Schuster.

Hughes, R. (1991). *The shock of the new: art and the century of change*. London: Thames & Hudson.

Imray, P. and Colley, A. (2017). *Inclusion is dead: long live inclusion*. Abingdon: Routledge.

Kauffman, J. M. and Hallahan, D. P. (1995). *The illusion of full inclusion: a comprehensive critique of a current special education bandwagon*. Austin, TX: Pro-Ed.

Kauffman, J. M. & Sasso, G. M. (2006a). Certainty, doubt, and the reduction of uncertainty. *Exceptionality*, 14(2): 109–120.

Kauffman, J. M. & Sasso, G. M. (2006b). Toward ending cultural and cognitive relativism in special education. *Exceptionality*, 14(2): 65–90.

Killoran, M. (2017). Pauline Hanson says that Autistic Kids should be Removed from the Mainstream Classroom. *The Courier Mail*, Brisbane, June 21st 2017 6.55pm. www.couriermail.com.au/news/queensland/pauline-hanson-says-autistic-kids-should-be-removed-from-mainstream-classes/news-story/9aca507ace3efc7 07dfa0d7648fc6180 (Retrieved June 25th 2017 13.10 AEST).

Knight, T. (1985). An apprenticeship in democracy. *The Australian Teacher*, 11(1): 5–7.

Kozol, J. (1991). *Savage inequalities: children in America's schools*. New York: Crown Publishers.

Kutchins, H. and Kirk, S. A. (1997). *Making US crazy. DSM: the psychiatric bible and the creation of mental disorders*. New York: Free Press.

Lawrence, D., Johnson, S., Hafekost, J., Boterhoven de Haan, K., Sawyer, M., Ainley, J., and Zubrick, S. R. (2015). *The mental health of children and adolescents: report of the second Australian child and adolescent survey of mental health and wellbeing*. Canberra: Department of Health.

Levitin, D. (2008). *The world in six songs*. New York: Dutton.

Levitin, D. (2016). *A field guide to lies and statistics*. New York: Viking an imprint of Penguin Books.

Malaquias, C. (2017). Three myths of special education – thoughts for parents. *Starting with Julius rganisation*, December 27th. www.startingwithjulius.org.au/3-myths-of-special-education-thoughts-for-parents/ (Retrieved February 2nd 2018 12:55am AEDT).

Marr, D. (2017). The White Queen: one nation and the politics of race. *Quarterly Essay*, 65: 1–102.

Meyer, H. and Benavot, A. (2013). *PISA, power & policy: the emergence of global educational governance*. Didcot: Symposium Books.

Milanović, B. (2016). *Global inequality: a new approach for the age of globalization*. Cambridge, MA: The Belknap Press of Harvard University Press.

Mitchell, D. T. and Snyder, S. L. (1997). *The body and physical difference: discourses of disability*. Ann Arbor, MI: University of Michigan Press.

Morrison, T. (2017). *The origin of others*. Cambridge, MA: Harvard University Press.

Morrison, V. (2014). I forgot that love existed. In E. Hughes (Ed.) *Lit up inside*. London: Faber & Faber.

Nussbaum, M. C. (2004). *Hiding from humanity: disgust, shame, and the law*. Princeton, NJ: Princeton University Press.

Nussbaum, M. C. (2006.) *Frontiers of justice: disability, nationality, species membership*. Cambridge, MA: The Belknap Press of Harvard University Press.

Oliver, M. (1990a). *The politics of disablement*. Basingstoke: Palgrave Macmillan.

Oliver, M. (2009b). *Understanding disability: from theory to practice*. Basingstoke: Palgrave Macmillan.

Oliver, M. and Barnes, C. (2012). *The new politics of disablement*. Basingstoke: Palgrave Macmillan.

Paris, J. and Phillips, J. (Eds.) (2013). *Making the DSM-5*. Dordrecht: Springer.

Parrish, T. (2005). Racial disparities in the identification, funding and provision of special education. In D. J. Losen and G. Orfield. (Eds.) *Racial inequality in special education*. Cambridge, MA: Harvard Education Press, pages 15–37.

Piketty, T. (2014). *Capital in the twenty-first century*. Cambridge, MA: The Belknap Press of Harvard University Press.

Ravitch, D. (2011). *The death and life of the great American school system: how testing and choice are undermining education*. New York: Basic Books.

Richardson, J, G., Wu, J., and Judge, D. M. ((2017). *The global convergence of vocational and special education.* New York: Routledge.

Rose, H. and Rose, S. P. R. (2013). *Genes, cells and brains: the promethean promises of the new biology.* London: Verso.

Rose, M. (1995). *Possible lives: the promise of public education in America.* Boston, MA: Houghton Mifflin Co.

Rose, N. (2007). *Politics of life itself: biomedicine, power and subjectivity in the twenty-first century.* Princeton, NJ: Princeton University Press.

Rose, N. and Abi-Rached, J. M. (2013). *Neuro: the new brain science and the management of the mind.* Princeton, NJ: Princeton University Press.

Rose, N. and Abi-Rached, J. M. (2014). Governing through the brain: neuropolitics, neuroscience and subjectivity. *Cambridge Anthropology,* 32(1): 2–23.

Rose, S. P. R. (2005). *The 21st-century brain: explaining, mending and manipulating the mind.* London: Jonathan Cape.

Ryan, W. P. (1971). *Blaming the victim.* London: Orbach & Chambers.

Sachs, J. (2006). *The end of poverty: economic possibilities for our time.* New York: Penguin Books.

Sacks, P. (1999). *Standardized minds: the high price of America's testing culture and what we can do to change it.* Cambridge, MA: Perseus Books.

Said, E. W. (2000). Travelling theory reconsidered. In E.W. Said (Ed.) *Reflections on exile and other literary and cultural essays.* London: Granta Publications, pages 436–452.

Salokangas, M. and Ainscow, M. (2018). *Inside the autonomous school: making sense of a global educational trend.* Abingdon: Routledge.

Sennett, R. (2006). *The culture of the new capitalism.* New Haven: Yale University.

Shaddock, A., Packer, S., & Roy, A. (2015). *Schools for all children and young people: report of the expert panel on students with complex needs and challenging behaviour.* Canberra: Australian Capital Territory Department for Education.

Shakespeare, T. (2006). *Disability rights and wrongs.* London: Routledge.

Shorter, E. (2013). The history of DSM. In J. Paris and J. Phillips (Eds.) *Making the DSM-5.* Dordrecht: Springer.

Sibley, D. (1995). *Geographies of exclusion: society and difference in the West.* London: Routledge.

Slee, R. (1993). The politics of integration – new sites for old practices? *Disability, Handicap & Society,* 8(4): 351–360.

Slee, R. (2011). *The irregular school.* Abingdon: Routledge.

Smith, A. (1759). *The theory of moral sentiment.* Part 1, Chapter 3. www.marxists.org/reference/archive/smith-adam/works/moral/part01/part1c.htm.

Snyder, S. L. and Mitchell, D. T. (2006). *Cultural locations of disability.* Chicago: University of Chicago Press.

Stiglitz, J. E. (2012). *The price of inequality: how today's divided society endangers our future.* New York: W.W. Norton & Co.

Stiker, H-J. (1999). *A history of disability.* Ann Arbor, MI: University of Michigan Press.

Stobart, G. (2008). *Testing times: the uses and abuses of assessment.* London: Routledge.

Titchkosky, T. (2007). *Reading and writing disability differently: the textured life of embodiment*. Toronto: University of Toronto Press.

Tobin, R. M. and House, A. E. (2016). *DSM-5 diagnosis in the schools*. New York: Guildford Press.

Tomlinson, S. (1981). *Educational subnormality: a study in decision-making*. London: Routledge & Kegan Paul.

Tomlinson, S. (1982). *A sociology of special education*. London: Routledge & Kegan Paul.

Tomlinson, S. (1985). The expansion of special education. *Oxford Review of Education*, 11(2): 157–165.

Tomlinson, S. (2013). *Ignorant yobs? Low attainers in a global knowledge economy*. New York: Routledge.

Tomlinson, S. (2017). *A sociology of special and inclusive education: Exploring the manufacture of inability*. Abingdon: Routledge.

Trump, D. (2015). *Crippled America: how to make America great again*. New York: Threshold Editions.

UNESCO (1994a). *Final report: world conference on special needs education: access and quality*. Paris: UNESCO, pages viii & ix www.unesco.org/education/pdf/SALAMA_E.PDF (Retrieved August 2nd 2017 13.26 AEST).

UNESCO (1994b). *The Salamanca statement and framework for action on special needs education*. Geneva: United Nations Educational, Scientific and Cultural Organisation, Madrid, Ministry of Education and Science Spain, Salamanca, Spain, June 7th–10th: ix, http://unesdoc.unesco.org/images/0009/000984/098427eo.pdf (Retrieved July 3rd 2017 10:17 AEST).

UNESCO (1999). *From special needs education to education for all: a discussion document*. Tenth Steering Committee Meeting UNESCO, Paris, September 30th–October 1th 1998. Unpublished manuscript.

United Nations (2006). *United nations convention on the rights of persons with disabilities and optional protocol (UNCRPD)*. New York. www.un.org/disabilities/documents/convention/convoptprot-e.pdf (Retrieved July 3rd 2017 1042 AEST).

Varoufakis, Y. (2016). *And the weak suffer what they must?* London: The Bodley Head.

Victoria Department of Education and Training (2016). *Review of the program for students with disabilities*. Melbourne: DET. www.education.vic.gov.au/Documents/about/department/PSD-Review-Report.pdf (Retrieved July 3rd 2017 15.09 AEST)

Walker, P. (2017). Report sparks concern about how schools support students with disabilities. *The Conversation*, June 13th 12.34 AEST. https://theconversation.com/report-sparks-concern-about-how-schools-support-students-with-disabilities-78753 (Retrieved July 4th 2017 18.53 AEST).

Walton, E. L. (2016). *The language of inclusive education: exploring speaking, listening, reading, and writing*. Abingdon: Routledge.

Warnock, M. (2005). *Special educational needs: a new look*. London: Philosophical Society of Great Britain. *Impact*, Number 11.

Watters, E. (2010). *Crazy like us: the globalization of the American psyche*. New York: Free Press.

Wendell, S. (1996). *The rejected body: feminist philosophical reflections on disability*. New York: Routledge.

Whitaker, R. G. (2002). *Mad in America: bad science, bad medicine, and the enduring mistreatment of the mentally ill*. Cambridge, MA: Perseus Publications.

Whitaker, R. G. (2010). *Anatomy of an epidemic: magic bullets, psychiatric drugs, and the astonishing rise of mental illness in America*. New York: Crown Publishers.

Wilkinson, R. G. and Pickett, K. (2010). *The spirit level: why equality is better for everyone*. London: Penguin.

Wills, G. (2015). *Zappa and Jazz: did it really smell funny Frank?* Kibworth: Beauchamp, Matador.

Wiltshire, K. (2017). Special needs education calls for cooperative effort. *Commentary, The Australian*, Sydney: Newscorp., July 1–2, page 22.

Wright Mills, C. (1959). *The sociological imagination*. New York: Oxford University Press.

Youdell, D. (2006). *Impossible bodies, impossible selves exclusions and student subjectivities*. Dordrecht: Springer.

Zappa, F. and Occhiogrosso, P. (1990). *The real Frank Zappa book*. London: Picador.

Zizek, S. (2016). *Disparities*. London: Bloomsbury.

Index

For Product Safety Concerns and Information please contact our EU representative GPSR@taylorandfrancis.com Taylor & Francis Verlag GmbH, Kaufingerstraße 24, 80331 München, Germany

Batch number: 08147289

Printed by Printforce, the Netherlands